"It's not often you read a ⎯⎯⎯⎯⎯⎯⎯⎯ that is as intimate and honest as *Send Me into the Woods Alone*. Pepler showcases her vulnerability and insight on every page, all salted with humour and relatability. As a parent you will identify with Pepler's personal journey through motherhood through her twenty-six essays. You will commiserate with some and be an observer on others. Either way, you will fully enjoy every word, knowing that you are not alone. Pepler's got you!"

— JANE BRADLEY, EDITOR OF *PARENTSCANADA*

"A kind and compassionate book that acknowledges all the emotional heavy lifting that is motherhood. *Send Me into the Woods Alone* is the perfect antidote to that guilt-inducing social media post that has you questioning every parenting decision you've ever made and/or your decision to become a parent at all. Erin Pepler understands the struggle and she's there to offer a well-timed message of encouragement, just when you need it most. Easily the most validating book you'll read this year."

— ANN DOUGLAS, AUTHOR OF *HAPPY PARENTS, HAPPY KIDS* AND *THE MOTHER OF ALL PREGNANCY BOOKS*

"Calling a collection of parenting essays *Send Me into the Woods Alone* is a stroke of genius, but Erin Pepler doesn't spend all of her truth-telling humor on the title. Her witty, warm stories will make you laugh in recognition at the absurd contradictions, frustrations, and complexities of modern motherhood/life in general. With a rare dry humor, Erin gives herself, and her reader, the space to—gasp!—complain about some of the less thrilling parts of parenting, and to acknowledge that it's always "okay to not feel okay." She even cheerfully recognizes the sheer boredom that we'd all like to pretend doesn't exist. (When I read, "Chutes and Ladders is not a game, it's a curse," I gave a silent cheer.) On the next page, though, you'll find yourself with a sudden lump in your throat when she deftly captures the mysterious, fierce love that, thankfully, also comes with the territory."

— APRIL DANIELS HUSSAR, MANAGING EDITOR OF *ROMPER*

"Erin Pepler's collection of honest, funny, and relatable essays is infused with hard-won wisdom and insights into the strange, difficult, and wonderful world of motherhood. Reading Pepler's essays is like hanging out with your best mom-friend—the one who puts it all out there, makes you feel normal, and has you laughing so hard you pee a bit."

— KIM SHIFFMAN, EDITOR-IN-CHIEF OF *TODAY'S PARENT*

"*Send Me into the Woods Alone* is one of the most supportive books on parenting I've ever read. It's insightful, heartwarming and oh-so-funny. This is a must-read for mothers."

— SHANNON LEE SIMMONS, AUTHOR OF *WORRY-FREE MONEY*

SEND
ME
INTO
THE
WOODS
ALONE

SEND
ME
INTO
THE
WOODS
ALONE

ESSAYS ON MOTHERHOOD

ERIN PEPLER

Invisible Publishing
Halifax & Prince Edward County

Library and Archives Canada Cataloguing in Publication
Title: Send me into the woods alone : essays / Erin Pepler.
Names: Pepler, Erin, author.
Identifiers: Canadiana (print) 20210347783
             Canadiana (ebook) 20210347821
             ISBN 9781988784892 (softcover)
             ISBN 9781988784939 (HTML)

Subjects: LCGFT: Essays.
Classification: LCC PS8631.E645 S46 2022 | DDC C814/.6—dc23

Edited by Andrew Faulkner
Cover and interior design by Megan Fildes | Typeset in Laurentian
With thanks to type designer Rod McDonald

Invisible Publishing is committed to protecting our natural environment. As part of our efforts, both the cover and interior of this book are printed on acid-free 100% post-consumer recycled fibres.

Printed and bound in Canada.

Invisible Publishing | Halifax & Prince Edward County
www.invisiblepublishing.com

Published with the generous assistance of the Canada Council for the Arts, the Ontario Arts Council, and the Government of Canada.

 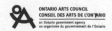 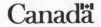

For OJP and HTP

AUTHOR'S NOTE

I began writing essays for this collection sometime in 2018, signed a contract with my publisher in the summer of 2019, and handed in a first draft of my manuscript in the spring of 2020. This timeline means that almost everything I've written in the next 200ish pages is from an era that a lot of us now refer to as the before times. Before the pandemic, before face masks and the great toilet paper shortage, before murder hornets and *Tiger King*. Before school closures and online drinks and Zoom fatigue. Back when parenting was just regular hard instead of pandemic hard.

There is a lot to say about the past two years, but I cannot and will not say it here. There is no way to adequately reflect on something that isn't over. *Send Me into the Woods Alone* was written pre-pandemic and this author's note is being written during the fourth wave. When the book hits shelves in the spring of 2022, things will likely be different than they are now—but how? I have no idea. I hope it's some sort of joyful post-pandemic rumspringa, but anything is possible. I used to use that phrase loosely, but these days, it feels extremely literal. Anything is possible.

So here we are, hopefully nearing the end of a pandemic, doing the best we can. I would like to say I'm hashtag vaxxed and relaxed but more realistically, I'm vaxxed and cautiously optimistic about the future. Things are bound to get better. I mean, it's not like billionaires are going to start flying to space for fun in the middle of a global health crisis, right? (Just kidding, that totally happened.)

What I will say is this: if your mental health suffered during this pandemic, you're not alone. If friendships and family relationships were tested, same. If you feel worn out and worn down, I hear you. My pandemic experience was dripping with privilege, and I still feel like that melty stub of a candle you should have tossed out months ago but keep trying to light anyway. Pretty much everyone admits they're burnt out. The rest are lying. This chapter of our lives has highlighted kindness and resilience but also exposed a lot of selfishness and an inability to put others first. It's been hard. And it's been really hard on moms.

I have never been more dedicated to protecting my kids' physical and mental health or spent more time with them, and somehow I've never felt like a worse mom. It's hard to make decisions about risk mitigation for months on end and not question at least some of your choices. I did my best, and I bet you did too. But wow, it wasn't fun.

I do see a light at the end of the tunnel. By the time this book is published, we could be talking about the pandemic in the past tense. Or maybe the world is still a dumpster fire. I truly do not know. I feel like I'm writing a letter to the future right now. Please tell me things are better. Did we have a launch party for this book? Do bookstores still exist? God, I hope so. If we aren't living as mutant sewer people, I'll be satisfied. The bar was reset in 2020 and my standards are no longer as high as they once were. Also, I might be making jokes as a coping mechanism because the pandemic is still very much a big deal, and I genuinely don't know what the next six months or year holds. Hopefully not a zombie apocalypse. Whatever it is, it can't be harder for moms than parenting through the pandemic. Thanks for reading along.

With love and gratitude and endless hope,
Erin

INTRODUCTION

In the beginning, my knowledge of pregnancy was rooted in miracles. First, there was the stork—a lie my parents never actually told me but one I internalized, thanks to the wonder of pop culture and cartoons. And then there was Jesus, the most miracley of miracles: the son of God, immaculately conceived and born in a barn, where he was showered with practical items for a newborn—frankincense and myrrh. Joseph, ever the good guy, wasn't the baby's father but stood by Mary anyway. Sweet, blessed Mary, who I later realized was not a woman when she gave birth, but a tween. Much like the classic eighties film *Dirty Dancing*—an important part of my formative years—Sunday school offers a lot for a young girl to unpack later in life. Spoilers: I eventually became an atheist, and Penny did not have appendicitis.

As a child of maybe seven or eight, I remember hearing about unexpected teen pregnancy and being incredibly confused. How did that sort of thing happen? After all, it seemed like a complicated and very deliberate process, this pregnancy thing. My knowledge was, of course, entirely scientific, and thoroughly glossed over. How does one "accidentally" end up with a penis inside of them, fertilizing the egg and making a baby? That shouldn't just *happen*. At some point, I worked up the courage to ask my mother, who awkwardly explained that people don't just have sex for reproduction but also for pleasure. This knowledge horrified me. I'd understood that people around me were guilty of having sex a handful of times in order to have children, but now I knew they were also doing it for fun. And before marriage!

This is what inadequate sexual education in school gets you.

Later, when my knowledge expanded to include science, facts, and actual experience in human relationships, the concept of pregnancy remained miraculous. Conceiving, gestating, and birthing a human is no joke—I've done it twice now, and the experience is far more magical than any stork or biblical story. And motherhood? I'm tempted to say there are no words—and yet, here we are and away I go, trying to articulate an experience that so many of us share but process in wildly variable, deeply different ways.

Miracles are beautiful, dirty, heartbreaking, painful, spectacular, and impossible to understand until you see one in action. And even then, you might never fully trust what you know to be real; you fumble through, doing your best and pretending you've got it all figured out. This is the essence of motherhood. This is parenting. And this is where it all begins.

THE MIRACLE OF LIFE AND OTHER FEATS OF STRENGTH

We're led to believe that pregnancy is the most natural thing in the world. It can also be among the weirdest things to ever happen to the human body. Whether you have an amazing, glowing, magical pregnancy or feel like human garbage for nine months, it's an objectively strange experience to grow a person inside your body with the expectation that you will somehow get that person out of your body, without dying, and then love them for the rest of your life, just like that.

Yes, this is how the human race has persisted for thousands of years, but there's a reason people make up stories about where babies come from: conception, pregnancy, and childbirth are extremely unappealing in many, many ways. Giving up control of your body can be a scary, anxious experience, and I've never felt as vulnerable as I did when I was pregnant or giving birth. Sex? I'm decidedly in favour. Babies? Love them. All of the stuff in between? A goddamn nightmare.

This isn't true for everyone. Each person's physical and emotional experience in pregnancy is different, which means when we talk about pregnancy, the conversation is always personal. Every journey to motherhood is unique— and uniquely affecting—for better or worse. In my social circle, I've watched friends get pregnant with ease, get pregnant after years of trying, get pregnant when they were not trying, get pregnant with medical intervention, and, several heartbreaking times, not get pregnant at all despite every effort to do so. I've held the hands of devastated friends who have lost a pregnancy, suffered a stillbirth, or given birth prematurely. I have friends who were surprised with twins (sometimes not completely unexpectedly, thanks to the incredible science of IVF) and friends who ended up adopting. In the end, no one should be judged on their journey to motherhood—instead, let us judge parents on things they can actually control, like how many superfluous and/or silent letters they add to their children's names.

Starting a family is an incredible experience, even when it feels absolutely awful. I had no problem conceiving but had two remarkably difficult pregnancies. This was mostly due to a fun condition called hyperemesis gravidarum, an intense, persistent nausea and vomiting in pregnancy that often tapers off early in the second trimester but will some-times last the entire forty weeks. Like mine did.

In those early weeks, throwing up felt like a badge of hon-our. I was doing a lot more of it than I'd expected to—I'm an overachiever—but I chalked it up as a sign things were going well with the baby. I'd read that nausea was an indi-cator of a healthy pregnancy, and severe morning sickness had been linked to above average intelligence in children, so I found vomiting strangely comforting. Sometimes, after a particularly bad bout of puking, I'd sit up defiantly and think to myself, *This baby is going to be a fucking genius*. Other times, I'd lie on the floor and cry.

Eventually, it became clear that I didn't have the usual morning sickness. I was puking upward of twenty times a day, losing weight instead of gaining, and was so tired and dizzy I could barely function. The first trimester finally passed, but the symptoms were never-ending. I threw up so violently, I tore a muscle in my stomach and popped blood vessels in my face. Every smell was torture, whether it was the compost bin or a lovely fruit tray a well-meaning friend had brought over. The scent of my own shampoo made me vomit. The anti-nausea medication I was prescribed made me sleep all day, but when I was awake, I was sick. It was horrific.

Near the end of my second pregnancy—a mere calendar year after the first one, because somehow I thought it was a great idea to repeat the experience—I started peeing my pants when I vomited. Not once or twice, mind you. Every single time. I peed myself more often than I ever imagined possible and was usually too sick and massively pregnant to even realize what had happened until I saw the puddle at my feet. As an added bonus, because we lived in a rental triplex in the city, we shared laundry with two other apartments. Those were the days.

"You tricked me," my landlord chided me one day when we ran into each other on the street. He had been attempting to collect rent from the couple below, who fought all night and smoked in the alley outside our bathroom window all day. (He failed. They paid their rent on their own schedule, and that was that.)

"Sorry, what?" I awkwardly replied, unsure of what he meant.

He pointed at my belly, amused. "There's going to be more of you living in that apartment soon, I guess?"

I nodded and in response politely asked the landlord to take care of the mice that were scurrying around the apartment at night. Our cat had just died, revealing a problem he'd been silently dealing with as we slept. My toddler had taken to pointing out signs of the rodent invaders by happily shrieking "Mice!" with a proud smile. Sometimes it seemed like general commentary or repetition, but other times she was pointing at actual mice—bold little fuckers who dared to cross the hardwood in daylight, sensing my pregnancy-induced weakness and my toddler's inability to stop them.

My pregnancies were particularly terrible in a way that many pregnancies are not, but it did reveal some broader truths. I learned very quickly that no matter how physically or emotionally challenging things become, if you complain about anything pregnancy-related, you will be seen as terribly ungrateful and may be told as much. You could be throwing up constantly and have awful sciatica, but did you know that some women can't have babies? (Yes, you did know that, and it breaks your heart, and now you feel terrible about yourself because you *can* have babies and obviously are not grateful enough for your functional womb.) Yeah, you're pregnant and feel miserable, but didn't you know what you were getting yourself into? Pregnant women vomit—it's a normal part of the process. Honestly, you just need to push through and stop whining about it (even if you're hospitalized and on IV fluids, which, let's be honest, just reeks of attention-seeking). You're so lucky to be pregnant, and countless women would trade places with you in a heartbeat—don't forget it!

I kept all of this in mind as I carried on vomiting, wetting my pants, and willing the mice to disappear.

These sentiments aren't wrong, of course. No kind person would deliberately complain about their pregnancy in front of someone struggling to conceive, or who has lost a baby, and we can't always know who those people are. I often try to step lightly when I don't know someone's story. That said, can we please agree that everyone should be allowed to express their struggles and reach out for emotional support without judgment? This should be true always, but particularly when talking about experiences of pregnancy.

If you ask a pregnant person how they're doing, let them answer honestly. They might feel terrible. They might be scared. Maybe they need to vent, or cry, or just admit out loud that pregnancy hasn't been the beautiful experience they wanted it to be. They might also be holding a lot of these things in because they know the kind of reaction they might get, and it's not worth it.

That was me—and if that's you, too, you already know the world isn't always kind to anyone who dares to admit how unpleasant pregnancy can be.

Here's how it works. When you are blessed with the impending miracle of life, you must accept that blessing with open arms and speak only of how beautiful it is. The only acceptable emotions to display during pregnancy are excitement and joy—anything else is considered shamefully selfish and unappreciative. You are having a baby, after all. Discomfort is your job now. You must float around serenely like the Virgin Mary, or at least one of those naked pregnant celebrities on a magazine cover, radiating goodness and maternal pheromones.

People can be unforgiving when you're pregnant. This is because some of them have never actually been pregnant, and some of them were pregnant so long ago they've forgotten the less-rosy side effects of child-bearing. Others are just jerks, and some mean well but are painfully clueless. These are the people who greet you with, "Wow, you're getting big!" or let you know how tired you look. And if you aren't sleeping at night because your body has morphed into a terrifying, swollen version of itself, and you need to pee every ninety minutes? They'll chuckle and patronizingly tell you it's good practice for when the baby arrives.

Pregnancy isn't all bad, of course, but judgment and dismissiveness force women to downplay their discomfort, minimizing their pain even when it's impossible to hide. It's not uncommon to hear an expectant mother say something like: "I can't wait to meet my baby. I feel really awful with heartburn and I'm not sleeping well, and I threw up my breakfast again today, but oh my gosh, the nursery is really coming together. I can't wait."

You say something less than purely joyful about your pregnancy and then add on two or three positives to show that you aren't a baby-hating monster who doesn't deserve the opportunity to gestate an adorable parasite. The kicker is that you really meant those good parts! You are practically bursting with them and felt them as much as, if not so much more than, you felt the negative parts. But you have to deploy the positive stuff strategically to prove your worth as a mother-to-be. It's twisted. By acknowledging the undesirable aspects of pregnancy, none of us are indicating that we'd rather not be pregnant or that we don't feel absolute joy and excitement about the impending arrival of the baby. We are *psyched* about the baby! We just hate heartburn and sciatica and vomiting.

Not everyone struggles through pregnancy like I did, and some mothers even feel guilty about how pleasant their experience was in comparison to others. Some people genuinely love being pregnant, and it's awesome if you have one of those magical pregnancies where you glow and feel amazing and don't throw up constantly—the unicorn pregnancy, if you will. I hear they're real, though I have yet to see proof. (One of my closest friends had a magical unicorn pregnancy, but then she had an episiotomy and broke her tailbone in childbirth, so it doesn't count.)

Maybe this is why people who thrive in pregnancy fascinate me. I don't mean that snarkily and, truthfully, I am jealous. They look awesome and I wanted very badly to be them. You know who I mean—the ones who grow perfect little basketball bellies while staying slender and toned in all other places. The ones with glowing, clear skin and energy for days. Who do prenatal yoga and somehow escape any sort of nausea or fatigue, even noting that they've never felt better or more confident in their body. The ones who talk about how they might become a surrogate one day, not only to help another family but to enjoy the experience again. The ones who feel empowered instead of powerless.

There are no words for how far away from this my pregnancy experience was, but I'm happy for the unicorns. Bless their toned, energetic little hearts. There they are, standing outside at golden hour, taking maternity photos and generally being awesome at (giving) life.

I have nothing against maternity photo shoots. I love seeing life's milestones celebrated and I'm a sucker for a nice glamour shot. Put a pregnant person in a floaty white dress in a field of lavender at sunset, and I'm the first person to like it on Facebook. Like like like, and I'll mean it. You're beautiful and it's totally cool if you want to document your pregnancy this way. I did not, but only because I resembled a sobbing, vomiting bridge troll while pregnant and have spent years trying to erase the memory.

In fact, there are almost no photos of me during either of my pregnancies. This wasn't on purpose, but people seemed to understand that I was vulnerable, sick, and miserable—with the exception of a brief period in the third trimester wherein I unexpectedly rallied and felt okay for a few weeks. Outside of that time frame, taking my photo would have served zero purpose other than as a record of how awful I felt.

Having a baby is a full-on carnival of biology, but it's worth it. If it weren't, the human race would have ended by now. If fifty percent of the population weren't such incredible powerhouses (even those of us who threw up and cried a lot), there would be no new people. It would be a tragedy of epic proportions.

My path to motherhood was not what I wanted or expected, and in many ways it was genuinely traumatic. Hyperemesis gravidarum is terrible and isolating, as are the many other challenging conditions faced during pregnancy. I will shout from the rooftops until everyone who has a bad pregnancy feels that they can do the same, honestly and without shame: it's okay to not feel okay. Pregnancy can be ugly and brutal. That said, I would do it all again a thousand times over to have my kids—without hesitation, with every fibre of my being. I felt that on the day they were born, I feel it now, and I even felt it back when they were inside my belly, slowly destroying me from the inside.

A miserable pregnancy is disappointing, but it's a temporary disappointment, one that's out of your control and completely unrelated to your success as a mother. Pregnancy does not define you, and it certainly isn't reflective of your ability to parent. It's a medical condition with a lot of emotional ties and societal pressure. Sometimes it sucks. But then you get through it, however simple or hard that may be, and it's over. You're a mom, and those infamous nine months can fade away in the rear-view of your mind. You can choose to look back on pregnancy with rose-coloured glasses—or never look back at all. And if you're still in the thick of it, just remember—this too shall pass. Sometimes quite literally, through your vagina, in the form of a human.

In all the ways my pregnancies disappointed me, my children have exceeded every hope and dream. They're better than I ever imagined they could be, and my heart swells knowing they're real and they're mine. My pregnancies were traumatic, but when I look back on my life, I won't be thinking of those days I spent heaving on the bathroom floor. I won't think about how many times I threw up or all the times I cried because things were so completely terrible. I'll think about my children, and the rest will fade away.

A MILLION HANDS IN ONE VAGINA

There is no easy way to tell a medical student that she's stabbing you from inside your vagina. It's a delicate subject, so to speak, and it's particularly hard when the medical student is a young, nervous woman who is trying her best to see if you're dilated while her supervisor, your borderline elderly male obstetrician, looks on. She's trying. He's waiting. You feel something sharp repeatedly jabbing your birth canal and hold your breath, trying to spare her the humiliation of knowing she's hurt you. Is she wearing fake nails, or maybe a ring? If so, that's a really prominent gemstone—not smooth like an opal but maybe a statement piece, modern and jagged. Whatever it is, you're sure it's breaking through her thin latex glove and will soon slice your insides. Oof. Checks like this are quick, you remind yourself, and it will be over soon. She pokes around, hesitantly asserts that you're not dilated at all yet, and removes her gloved hand from your lady garden. Finally. You breathe deeply and relax.

Your doctor then throws on gloves and checks you again, of course, to see if the student was right. This time it doesn't hurt—not that it's pleasant to have an old man's hand up in your box, but his fingers are free of jabby objects and his approach far more confident and efficient. In and out, yup, not dilated. Well done, intern. They thank you for consenting to the additional check. This is how doctors learn, of course! You smile and nod. No problem. Another prenatal appointment in the books.

Oh, vaginas. Many people won't even say the correct name for that body part out loud, and then one day you find yourself in a dark ultrasound room, wondering how a fancy medical dildo is the only way to look for an early fetal heartbeat. That, my friends, is what I was thinking about when I was told there was a baby in me.

My due date changed several times, so near the end of my first pregnancy, around the time of the aforementioned appointment with the intern, it all felt like a guessing game. I knew I'd been pregnant for approximately nine months, so I assumed an infant was going to make an appearance soon. I was tired of constantly throwing up and feeling like garbage, and looked forward to being able to tie my own shoes again without Herculean effort. My breathing was laboured from walking and my hips ached from sciatica and a pinched nerve. I limped when I moved, my limbs were swollen, and, no matter how exhausted I was, I couldn't sleep unless I was propped up with an elaborate arrangement of pillows to thwart my acid reflux and keep the hip pain from flaring up. When I did fall asleep, I'd wake up to pee fifty times, carefully rearranging my pillow pile after every trip to the washroom. When morning came, the vomiting would start again. People spoke of labour as being a real ordeal, but I figured it couldn't be half as bad as my pregnancy. Or maybe it would be, but at least then the pregnancy would be over. Either way, I was ready to get the show on the road.

And so, when labour finally started, I was thrilled. *Get this baby out of me*, I thought. *Just please don't let me poop, tear, or require an episiotomy.*

It may seem strange that these were the things I feared the most about labour, but they're reasonable concerns. Someone had casually mentioned to me that my OB reportedly "loved" episiotomies, and countless friends had shared stories of tearing, which didn't sound any better. Very few admitted to pooping while pushing, but according to every pregnancy book, it was totally plausible. As a woman who has never passed gas in front of her husband, I found this possibility particularly horrifying. "If it happens, it happens," my husband said, shrugging. He's been free with his bodily functions from the early days of dating, whereas I've held in a single fart for a three-hour car ride and cannot even say the word aloud. I shook my head emphatically. "I'd die if I pooped in labour. I would just divorce you right then and there, so we'd never have to acknowledge it again."

It was with this mindset that I instructed my husband to remain near my shoulders during the birth. "I want you to have the same view I'm going to have," I explained. "Like a movie birth—where I'm pushing and you stand there and encourage me, and then the baby emerges from under the sheets, in the doctor's hands. There's no reason for you to see my birthing vagina. It's not the same as a sex vagina. I'd like to have sex again, eventually, and for us both not to have a visual reference of the train wreck of the birthing vagina. Please."

My husband was amused, but he agreed.

I wasn't afraid of giving birth, but I still didn't want my husband to see it happen up close, nor did I want to witness the gore myself. I could breathe through contractions, bear down, and push like a champion, but I didn't want to see the baby crowning or be distracted by the reflection of my anus in a birthing mirror. I was certain my body would come through and get the baby out safely, but I was far more comfortable feeling things happen than seeing them dead-on. A year or two before my first child was born, I'd had my gallbladder removed. The idea of surgery hadn't stressed me out, but if you'd asked me to stay conscious and watch the procedure in a mirror, I would have firmly declined. Sure, a baby is not a gallbladder, but I feel like the same theory applied. I didn't need to see things from the same angle as my obstetrician. I like to feel in control of my body, and I also like to deliberately avoid things that freak me out. Is that too much to ask?

When I noticed mild, steady contractions one Wednesday morning, I hopped on the subway and went to my weekly OB appointment, conveniently scheduled for that same day. My OB checked me, noted that I was a centimetre dilated, and agreed that I was in the early stages of labour. "So I'm going to have the baby today?" I asked excitedly. "Probably tomorrow," he replied, with the gentle expertise of a man who has seen several thousand cervixes. He explained that I was progressing slowly and should rest at home for as long as I could. He also suggested that I eat and take a nap while I was still comfortable, so I'd have energy later on. I called my husband, bought a bagel, a chicken noodle soup, and an iced cappuccino from the Tim Hortons in the hospital lobby, and decided I could justify a cab ride home. I was in labour, after all.

The next morning, the contractions were frequent and much stronger but still bearable. I was in significant pain, but not agony. "Do we go to the hospital?" my husband asked. I didn't know. The contractions were getting closer together and lasted longer, but I'd expected worse. Still, it seemed reasonable to check in on things. We went to the hospital, optimistic that we'd be told labour was moving along well.

I was greeted by nurses and led to a small room where they would check my dilation. Memories of the ringed intern flashed through my mind, and a young doctor I'd never seen before snapped on his glove and reached for my cervix. A gush of liquid flowed onto the hospital bed, and we locked eyes. "It's not pee," I said meekly. He nodded in awkward agreement: "Your water just broke. You're only about a centimetre dilated though. Maybe two. You can go home for now and come back in twelve hours or when your contractions are less than five minutes apart."

Come back in twelve hours? Sure, I've already been in labour for a full business day, but whatever. Dilation was not a race I was winning, and I wanted another iced cappuccino. (Truly, I cannot understate how many cold, blended drinks I consumed while pregnant. One of the few things that would temporarily stave off my nausea, they were my lifeblood.)

My contractions were already around five minutes apart, but I heard "two centimetres" and went home, certain I'd be pregnant forever. I was incredibly wrong. Within the hour, I was doubled over, gasping in pain, cursing the doctor and my husband and everyone I'd ever known. Lying down hurt and bouncing on the yoga ball was hell, so I tried the shower. When the water hit my back, I felt moderately better. More importantly, I felt calm.

This is how I found myself labouring alone in the shower for several hours, pained but content. My husband checked on me often and timed my contractions as they got closer together. Twelve hours after my water broke— over twenty-four hours since my OB appointment and the approximate start of my labour—I agreed to go back to the hospital. We called a cab.

I had not anticipated how awful it would feel going from standing in my hot shower to sitting in the back seat of a cold, bumpy taxi. The hospital was only ten minutes away without traffic, but snow had started to fall and, as luck would have it, it was rush hour. The pain seemed to double in a matter of minutes, and I soon found myself quietly whimpering in agony, writhing like an injured animal as we crawled along. My husband put on a brave face and assured me we'd be there soon. The cab driver, however, was not as confident.

He quickly tapped a series of numbers into his cellphone and began speaking Arabic in a low, concerned voice. The words "pregnant" and "baby" leapt out at me in English, and as the call became more animated, I realized that he thought I was going to give birth in the cab. He looked back at me in the rear-view mirror, his voice raising in both volume and pitch as he spoke into the phone. "I'm fine!" I squeaked out, my fists clenched in pain. My torso felt like it was being ripped apart by sharks, but I felt no urge to push and was sure we'd make it to the hospital. "Don't worry, these things take a while." He drove fast and aggressively, even for a cab driver, and eventually screeched to a halt in front of Mount Sinai Hospital, where I myself had been born. I have never seen relief like the look on that cabbie's face when I stepped out of his car, still pregnant, having not given birth in his vehicle. We tipped him well, as one does when they scar a person for life. (I'm sorry, cab driver.)

Another doctor, another hand in my vagina, and then the proclamation that I was—get this—two centimetres dilated. "But...I was two centimetres over twelve hours ago," I protested, barely able to speak through the pain. "My water broke *this morning* and I'm *dying*. Like, it doesn't stop, it's just pain and then worse pain." Sympathetic but busy and not entirely convinced I was accurately describing my pain, the medical staff asked if I wanted an epidural. I nodded, abandoning the idea of a non-medicated birth. Whatever drugs they had, I wanted—all of them, as quickly as possible, straight into my veins. Plans change and choice is good.

While epidurals aren't for everyone, I will tell you this: they are for me. After a few misses with the needle and a brief period wherein only one side of my body was numb, the pain all but disappeared. Soon after, I was lying comfortably under a blanket, listening to my iPod and praising modern medicine. The music was great for relaxing and letting my body rest, and also for drowning out the sounds coming from the next room. My hospital neighbour, a stronger woman than I who had chosen not to take the epidural when offered, let out a steady stream of long, guttural moans. It sounded like a bear had been shot and left to die slowly in the woods—or two inebriated gorillas attempting to make love in the echoing mountains. The sound vibrated through the thin hospital walls and continued for hours, worsening as the night went on. I turned up the volume in my headphones and hoped her baby would come soon.

Being numb from the ribs down was pleasant, and also made the parade of hands inside my vagina over the next few hours easier to tolerate. Oh hey, person I've never seen before but who is apparently the doctor in charge right now, you want to check my cervix? Go for it, let me know what's up. Student doctor who needs to cop a feel so she can learn? Sure, get in there. The hours went on and my labour seemed to be frozen in time—more checks, very little progress. Shifts changed and new hands explored my nether region, always with the same news: not much dilation was happening. They hooked me up to an IV of Pitocin and promised things would speed up.

Fortunately, they were right. When I finally hit full dilation approximately fifty hours into my labour, the doctor had an epiphany. "Oh!" she said. "This baby is posterior. She's face up and has been stuck behind your pelvic bone—that explains why you weren't dilating." It also meant she might continue to be stuck there as I pushed, which resulted in a quick debriefing on forceps, vacuums, and other possible interventions.

"I don't want an episiotomy!" I insisted. The doctor promised she'd do her best to avoid one, quietly noting that a C-section was probably a bigger concern. Tables and medical carts were set up, nurses sprang into action, and the doctor reached back up inside me to check the baby's position. By now, I barely noticed when someone was wrist-deep in my lady bits—it would have been weirder had someone not been in there, honestly. This time I got good news.

The doctor locked eyes with me with the intensity of a high school football coach on game day. "This is *not* a big baby. Listen to me—you're going to be fine." I nodded, and then pushed with all my might.

Less than ten minutes later, I was a mom. Weighing in at just over five pounds, my tiny daughter was immediately my favourite person on the planet. I barely noticed as the doctor threw me a handful of stitches before giving us some alone time as a family of three.

What's interesting about childbirth is that, unlike pregnancy, we're allowed to acknowledge how gross it is. Complain about your pregnancy? Shame on you, lady. Mention that you had a rough labour and delivery? Watch the sympathy roll in. Everyone knows that giving birth is the worst and anyone who's done it is a superhero. Yes, delivering a baby is a wonderful miracle of the human body, but it's also super painful, occasionally disgusting, and marks the beginning of a postpartum aftermath no one truly prepares you for. Have you ever seen an umbilical cord in real life? It looks like a gigantic, pulsating tapeworm that's attacking your newborn. It's messed up, and then they ask your husband to cut it with scissors, which is even wilder. They actually cheered my husband on like he was about to christen a boat, and then praised him for cutting the thing successfully. A woman spends over nine months gestating a child and then labours to birth it, guided through the process by a dedicated medical professional. At what point did someone suggest the father be given some sort of ceremonial role involving blood and scissors? Do men really need to feel important at every event? Maybe just sit back and let women have this one thing.

There is no denying how incredible it is that our bodies create and grow humans, and later release them from whence they came. I cannot whistle and sometimes say, "Righty tighty, lefty loosey," in my head when opening a jar, but somehow I've managed to push two small humans out of my vagina without completely destroying my body. Nature is amazing and so is medical science, and even so, childbirth is still a total shot in the dark. After all of this, my second labour was textbook—a slow build of contractions, steady dilation, a quick transition, and some pushing. A walk in the park, relatively speaking. I've said I could give birth to my son every weekend if I had to, and I mean it—the experience was so calm and easily manageable, it almost felt like cheating. Maybe birth isn't *always* the worst, I learned. (My son himself is not a reflection of his birth story—he may have ridden in on a gentle wave but he's a hurricane of a boy who has never, ever been described as "easily manageable.")

But back to my box, and the million hands I got to know so intimately. The day my daughter was born, there were exponentially more unique pairs of hands in my vagina than I've had sexual partners in my entire life. Manicured hands, wrinkled hands, young intern hands, hands I don't even remember. Hands that knew what they were doing and hands that used my body as a learning tool. A million hands in my one vagina. It was fine, because I consented to it and felt respected throughout the process. At no point did I feel uncomfortable or regret choices that were made. That's not everyone's experience, but it was mine—though on some level, I feel like maybe I should have at least tried to remember their faces.

WHEN THE BABY SNATCHER IS YOU

I remember the time I stole a baby from the hospital and took her home with me. It was easy—too easy, if you ask me—and altogether a fairly casual experience. No alarms went off, no doctors or security guards followed us in hot pursuit, and before I knew it, I was sitting at home with a latte in hand and a newborn baby in my lap. My only question was what to do next.

The baby was mine, but the feeling that I'd stolen her from the hospital was very real. After all, babies are serious business, and there I was with my accomplice/husband in our apartment, staring at a child we'd only met the day before but were now somehow expected to raise to adulthood. It felt magical but also baffling. I'd wanted this baby forever but never even owned a car. How had we gotten away with this?

Hours earlier, we'd been holed up in a comfortable yet unmistakably clinical room that felt like a cross between a hotel and a prison: white walls, bleached linens, generic art prints, and the underlying smell of urine and disinfectant. We got used to the authoritative thud of nurses' footsteps in the hall and the low, persistent beeps of machines. A thick hum of white noise was occasionally interrupted by the rattling of a janitorial cart or a new baby's cries. Sometimes the crying came not from the baby but from an excited grandparent or emotional aunt. The rooms were orderly and numbered, each new mother's name and medical details noted on a chart beside their door. A sign in the hallway reminded nurses to smile and be kind, which made me skeptical of every nice thing they said. Our sweet baby, wrapped in a soft pink flannel blanket, slept peacefully in a plastic bassinet. I was sore and exhausted but blissfully happy, even as I struggled to walk to the bathroom and change my metre-long sanitary pad.

Once my epidural wore off and I proved I was capable of both walking and using the washroom independently, we were told it was time to go home. I'd successfully breastfed the baby a few times, which apparently meant we'd be okay in the real world, and our hospital room was needed for the next wobbly-legged new mother and her offspring. We buckled our tiny, five-pound daughter into her car seat and walked out into the hallway as a newly formed family of three.

It felt insane. With every step, I waited to be questioned or asked for ID. I wanted to prove the baby was mine and what I was doing was, in fact, totally okay. That I wasn't a baby snatcher who'd stolen this perfect infant from the nursery. There wasn't even a nursery in that particular hospital, but where there's a will, there's a way to steal a baby, I'm sure.

Why wasn't there some sort of infant-customs process like the booths at airport terminal exits? This event felt far more momentous than getting off a plane—I couldn't possibly walk in pregnant and walk out with a human. She didn't even look like me, with her bald head and tiny fingers. This could be anyone's baby, and nobody seemed to care. I stepped out the back door of the hospital, took a deep breath, and headed toward the parking lot. Away we went.

Pregnancy and childbirth are complex experiences that are often well-monitored, but care in the aftermath is startlingly low-key. Once the baby is out, you simply go home and live your life like you always have—*but with a baby*. Holy shit, it's intense. Even when things go well, it's a radical shift. And when things are hard, they're really fucking hard.

I was lucky. After a miserable pregnancy and a fairly challenging labour, I felt great once we were back home. My first-born child was a dream: sweet, snuggly, and hardly ever fussy. She rarely cried and we could take her anywhere, from friends' houses to quiet restaurants. We took her to pubs where elderly couples would coo at her over plates of fish and chips. I'd pop her into her stroller or an infant carrier and wander all over the city, stretching my legs and running errands or relaxing in the park. It was idyllic. It wasn't the typical newborn experience, but I didn't really know that at the time. Oh man, it was great.

What a fool I was for not knowing how rare this effortless serenity is. While my pregnancies were cautionary tales that might scare people off having kids forever, those newborn days were unrealistically tranquil. If someone had made a documentary of my life in the early weeks and months at home with my first kid, it would have been panned for being a fanciful lie.

Other babies scream for hours on end, their bodies raging with colic. New mothers are tired, sore, and still healing from the C-sections that split them open only weeks earlier. As friends and neighbours fawn at newborns in their strollers, mothers are bleeding into adult diapers, their nipples rough and shooting with pain. "Yes, she's a great baby," they'll respond with a tired smile, and they mean it. All babies are good babies—there are just some who happen to wail for the first six months (or longer) of their lives.

Motherhood on the whole is wildly variable, and the newborn days are no exception. And yet, we're all sent out into the world the same way—to figure things out on our own, more or less. After months of attentive monitoring and care at the hands of a midwife or obstetrician, and then a birth aided by whatever medical assistance we wanted (or needed), we're suddenly not patients anymore. We become caretakers—we are Mom, Mama, Mommy, Mother, Ma, repeated over and over again, forever. But who takes care of mothers as their hormones shift and their bodies change, and their lives are dramatically, irrevocably altered? Even when things are wonderful, as they were for me, everything is also brand new. You cannot *not* adapt. There is no status quo.

Every decision you've ever made about your own body, lifestyle, and well-being, you now make for someone else: what to eat, how to spend the days, what to wear, who to spend time with, when to sleep (on this, you can only try). From the momentous to the inconsequential, you're the one calling the shots.

Reading the ingredient list on a box of infant oat cereal in the grocery store, I'd wonder if it was as full of arsenic as the Internet told me rice cereal was. The smiling baby on the box looked fine, but would I be doing permanent damage to my own child by feeding it to her? It was either vitamin-rich infant nutrition or poisonous processed swill, depending on who I listened to.

I opted to steam and puree dozens of vegetables, sprinkling a touch of cinnamon or ginger to make it more palatable, instead of buying the rice cereal. Cauliflower got a touch of coriander, and broccoli was sweetened with apple and pears. What a good mom I was, handcrafting baby food and lovingly building her palate. I was almost aggressive in my offering of the food pyramid—healthy proteins, fresh produce, a touch of something from the spice cupboard. She'd wash it down with twenty minutes on the boob and pass out, a satisfied baby lump.

But sometimes I was tired or busy and she was hungry, so she got plain oatmeal from a box. She loved it, obviously—most babies are happy with a bowl of warm, carby mush. I pushed aside thoughts of guilt, handing her hand-crushed blueberries to compensate. We'd have lentils and sweet potato tomorrow, I reasoned—this was just a break in our routine. I painstakingly plotted out my children's food intake, and it worked. They happily eat their veggies to this day. Oh, and they also love french fries, candy, and chicken nuggets because while I agonized over that grain cereal years ago, I eventually gave in to drive-through meals and other conveniences of parenting. As it turns out, this hasn't ruined my kids.

These are the things we don't always consider when we're making decisions for our babies—they may be eating homemade squash puree now, but one day you'll be at a birthday party and see them shooting back a Pixie Stix, and you'll think, *Fuck it, there's no going back now. It's a party— let them have it.*

Those early days were almost too easy. I agonized over oat cereal and very little else. The choices I made were not life or death, and rarely did I do more than follow my instincts. If I could have frozen time, I would have.

But I am not every mom—not even close.

My mind goes to the new mom who sits in a dark, lonely room, fighting postpartum demons in her head and wondering why her mind and body won't co-operate. Whose breasts sear with pain though no milk comes, whose mind races and whose nerves are stuck in fight-or-flight mode. Who cannot keep her eyes open but also cannot fall asleep. Who questions every decision she makes. Whose baby cries and cries and cries, but she can't figure out why or how to make them stop. The moms who are overwhelmed, under-supported, or just plain scared. And the many, many moms who hide some or all of this because society demands motherhood should be beautiful and wonderful, and that good moms don't get overwhelmed.

These are the women we fail, because for every mother who has an amazing partner, friend, or doctor to help them through, there's one who slips through the cracks. The mom who suffers in silence. One woman who feels lost and alone in motherhood is one woman too many.

I didn't always see these women because I wasn't one of them. Blinded by my own serene post-birth existence, I didn't stop and ask how my new mom friends were coping with their changing lives. They loved their babies as much as I loved mine—that was plain to see—and I was sure they were fine. Until they started talking.

First, one confessed how much she hated breastfeeding. It hurt, it wasn't working, she couldn't produce enough milk to adequately feed her child. She felt like a failure—if she pushed on, she'd be miserable, and her baby still might not get enough. If she switched to formula, she'd be a quitter at the mercy of mom-shamers. She felt broken.

Another friend timidly asked a few women in her play group if they ever felt a strong desire for someone else to hold their baby. Like, anyone else. "I just can't have her in my arms all the time anymore," she confessed. "I don't want to. I just need a break from nursing and holding and soothing. I need to go somewhere without her." She was near tears at the admission that she, an adult human, might want to use her arms freely or leave the house alone every once in a while. Her shame was palpable when a few of the mothers around her stared blankly in response. "I've never felt that way," one said coldly. My friend was crushed.

When a woman has overt postpartum depression or psychosis, we think of it as an extreme and sad case. We're empathetic, maybe, but it's not something that happens to all mothers, and we see their struggles as isolated cases. It's not that bad for everyone, but for a lot of people, being a new mom can be as agonizing as it is joyous. It's just that until it's so bad it can't be ignored, it gets ignored.

Even in my bliss, I had moments of crushing anxiety. There were times I was so sleep-deprived and exhausted I could barely think straight, let alone hold up my end of a conversation. I may have been calm and happy ninety percent of the time, but cluster-feeding left me raw and touched out. My body often felt like it belonged to my child more than it did to me. I wasn't at risk of self-harm, but more support would have been lovely, had it been available.

I would have liked to shower alone or eat a hot meal. You don't need to be drowning to appreciate a life jacket.

No matter how naturally motherhood comes to some of us, how much we love our children, or how "easy" our kid is, having a new baby is like being thrown to the wolves. An arduous physical, mental, and emotional journey begins the moment our first child is born, if not sooner, and it never ends. It's like starting a new job with minimal training and zero experience for a boss with sky-high expectations—plus everyone you know is watching from the sidelines. Despite this, we've been conditioned to think that motherhood is instinctive, something all women fall into with grace as soon as we're settled at home post-delivery.

There's a reason I felt like I was stealing my baby that day at the hospital: I guess I expected more fanfare. Taking a child home turns your world upside down, for better and for worse, and it's harder to buy beer than it is to exit a hospital with a newborn. It felt like I'd missed several steps along the way.

The birth of your baby is treated as an end goal, except we all know it's just the beginning, as if giving birth is the peak in the motherhood journey and everything thereafter is a pleasant reward. It's not. Rewarding, sure, but it's not a gentle downhill stroll. From the moment you become the baby-snatcher, you are responsible for more than you ever have been in your life.

When I looked down at my newborn latched on to me, eyes closed, wispy hairs atop a perfect head, I was in heaven. I'd watch them breathe and smile in their sleep, soaking in their warmth and that new-baby smell. Honestly, there's nothing like feeling your child's head nestled in the crook of your neck, purring sleepily beside your ear as they drift off. I drank them in. But now I see the other side—the new mothers who struggle to keep their heads above water. Who just want to survive this stage. The mothers whose experiences are so different from mine, but just as valid.

When you walk out into the bright sun with your newborn baby nestled in a car seat, looking for the getaway car and hoping you're home before any sirens wail, I hope there are people there to hold your hand. To make you a warm meal, let you shower in peace, and tell you that everything is going to be okay, especially when you feel like it won't. If your days are mostly joy-filled and magical, I hope you soak that in—and if they're not, know it's okay. It's normal. You may not have actually stolen a baby, but you're officially a mom, and that's just as wild.

LULLABIES FROM POP RADIO

My children love Elvis, and they don't even know it. In this same blissfully unconscious way, they love Leonard Cohen, Bob Marley, and Brandi Carlile. They would never recognize Coldplay by name, but they know "Green Eyes" when it begins, beckoning them with its gentle chords and simple, earnest lyrics.

At night, after I read them stories and tuck them into bed, my kids ask me to sing them a song. And because I don't like children's music—a crime in some circles, I know—I sing them the songs of pop stars and indie balladeers: Taylor Swift, Patti Griffin, Billie Eilish, Feist. I sing mournful love songs by City and Colour and songs about whisky by Chris Stapleton. Sometimes they drift off to sleep while I fake my way through an Ed Sheeran song they've requested or a Bryan Adams classic I've insisted upon—"Heaven" is the perfect lullaby.

Their top pick is "Hallelujah" by Leonard Cohen but sung like Jeff Buckley as attempted by me, though Elvis is a close second. They might not be able to pick Elvis out of a lineup—pictured young or old or anywhere in between—but they'll sweetly tell me they want to hear "wise men" and I know what to do, leading off with a line about fools rushing in.

If my children and I have a song, it's "Can't Help Falling in Love." It is our love song, quietly breaking through the darkness night after night. I have sung it more than I can remember, often in the croaky, strained voice of someone who is lying down on a single bed with a child jammed up against her throat, and other times with slightly more grace. It is a song that brings them comfort and calm, even if they have no idea what the original sounds like. As far as my kids are concerned, it's something I produce like a warm blanket at the end of the day.

I love singing to them, but I don't like to sing in front of other people. It makes me feel vulnerable and naked, and generally I refuse to do it. I have done karaoke exactly once (on a rare occasion when I was drunk) and my throat tightened up in fear, creating a sound not unlike an unwell bird. But with my kids, I'm uninhibited: I sing my heart out, albeit quietly enough that the sound doesn't travel too far beyond their bedrooms. I don't want an audience beyond my children—they are the only audience that matters.

Every once in a while, my son will ask to sing with me. As we're curled up together among his stuffed animals, he'll indicate he's ready and then launch into "Hallelujah" with so much tenderness I am almost painfully overwhelmed by my love for him. It's a privilege to have a child sing with you in complete earnestness and contentment. He sings in perfect melody and rhythm, his tiny six-year-old voice so sweet and pure, even when he gets the words wrong or skips a verse. When he's done—or he ends the song because he's forgotten how the rest of it goes—he asks the same question: "Do you like my singing, Mama?"

"I do," I tell him. "I love your singing."

"You're my favourite singer in the world," he always tells me back. Before I can tell him how much that means to me, he might lean back into his pillow and ask for "Baby don't worry about a thing." I oblige and launch into my rendition of "Three Little Birds."

One day, my children won't want me to sing for them anymore. They'll be too cool, or too aware of the intimacy created by listening to someone you love sing up close, and they'll stop asking. Age and reticence and a growing need to put emotional distance between us will end this tradition; it'll become something we did rather than something we do, and my heart will ache just a little.

My hope is that one day, when my children are grown and off living a life away from me, they might think back fondly on those moments in our bedtime routine. That maybe they'll be off at college and hear "Three Little Birds" at a party, or "Can't Help Falling in Love" will come on the car radio, and they'll experience that visceral burst of memory that sound can elicit. That maybe they'll think of me singing them to sleep night after night. I hope it reminds them of how much they're loved.

Looking into the future is fruitless, but it can still be sweet. By the time my kids are out of high school or off working jobs, there might not even be radio as I think of it now—at the rate things are going, music will probably be streamed directly into their brains by then—but the songs and the memories will remain. I'll be there, in one form or another, always ready to sing another chorus while rubbing their backs in time with the melody: gently, lovingly, until their breaths deepen, and they're safely lost in sleep. And one day, when I am just a memory to them, I hope these songs bring them comfort again. In the meantime, I'll keep singing.

EVERYONE LIES ON THE INTERNET

There are many things to be said about how the Internet has reshaped the world and how it's affected our perception of the people who live in it. Over the last few decades, we've gone from worrying about our own lives to staring at everyone else's, albeit through curated feeds that are as ripe with illusion as they are with truth. The Internet is a weird portal that's opened up countless doors and slammed others shut, leaving us with a wildly distorted sense of reality. I like to think of the Internet as a kitchen knife: it's a helpful tool with plenty of uses, if you know what you're doing and how to handle it with care—but if you don't pay attention, you'll end up bleeding all over the place. (If you think this is dramatic, you've never been in a mommy group on Facebook.)

Each and every week during both of my pregnancies, I received an email telling me which fruit my baby was the size of, along with a series of charming and terrifying medical facts. (In week twelve, they are the size of a lime and grow earlobes!) I've never known motherhood without Facebook mom groups and a million blogs that delve into everything from vaginal prolapses to nursery aesthetics. I can google anything I'd ever want to know about pregnancy, childbirth, or motherhood, and within seconds I have access to a thousand opinions on the subject. This is useful, and it's absolutely overwhelming.

Social media has come to dictate what motherhood should look like—and if that's not how motherhood looks for you, you've gone wrong somewhere along the way. It's a breeding ground of comparison, vanity, and shame, and one of the main reasons competitive parenting is so firmly entrenched in our lives.

It also makes us feel inadequate. A really sweet mom at my kids' school once told me that I'm her idea of "mom goals" because I clearly have my shit together while she feels like a scatterbrained moron. "You always know what's going on at the school and pack these great lunches and volunteer on field trips and give awesome teacher gifts even though you're working, and I have no idea when there's an assembly or what's going on," she said with a laugh. "And your kids are so smart! You're doing things right." I was flattered, but also completely shocked that this woman, who had known me for several years by this point, didn't realize what a hot mess I was. Why not? Because she follows me on social media, where I share pictures of those awesome lunches and teacher gifts and very rarely post about all the times I drop the ball.

But here's the full truth: I volunteer on field trips because I have anxiety and am convinced something bad is going to happen to my kids if I'm not there. I make really good lunches for the kids, but I suck at taking care of myself and usually eat a piece of banana bread in my car or have left-overs at my desk at two in the afternoon because I realize I haven't had anything but coffee all day.

I know what's going on at school because I'm a control freak who needs information to feel safe and I have a hard time saying no when asked to volunteer. I give awesome teacher gifts because I genuinely like the teachers but also because I want them to like me back and be nice to my kids.

My house is a mess, and the inside of my car looks like the dumpster behind a Starbucks. I make sure my kids are clean and well-dressed, but some days I don't brush my own hair. I'm good at my job, but I often work really long hours and don't sleep enough, which makes me irritable. I take my kids to piano and swim lessons every week, but we're late for school all the damn time. The secretary definitely hates me.

My kids are really smart, but one of them gets in trouble on a regular basis because he's the kind of smart that doesn't fit well into a traditional school system, and sometimes he gets into fights or, in his zest for life, accidentally breaks things. My other kid is Type A like me and really hard on herself and once cried because she didn't get perfect on a spelling test.

I said all of this to that mom at my kids' school, almost begging her to see how much of a glorious train wreck I am. I could have gone on forever, listing all my faults that this woman clearly didn't see. I stared at her glossy, freshly blow-dried hair and well-behaved children and wondered how she could possibly see me as a role model. Her house is immaculate, and I know she has a great job. Her husband is a wonderful guy, and she is among the nicest moms at the school. She was basically living in a Hallmark movie. What the hell was her problem, thinking I had my life together?

"Well, I think you're nailing it and you're still my mom goals," she replied, unmoved by my confessions. I brushed this off but still thanked her for noticing how hard I try.

The Internet isn't real life. It's basically a costume party. Social media is fun, but even when we're honest and "real," there's still a performative element to what we post. At its heart, social media is just a series of platforms designed to sell us things, from actual products to aesthetics and opinions, and we're all just selling something back.

Scrolling through Instagram on any given day, I see a ton of perfectly posed, heavily filtered, highly coordinated images designed to entice me. People and companies want me to want the outfit, the house, the body. They're influencing, with or without a paycheque, and I'm taking it all in. Even accounts that promise an unfiltered look at someone's life, or encourage you to love yourself despite your flaws, are selling a story (and often at least one product). I swear up and down that I represent myself honestly on social media, but I still decide what you see and what you don't. I'm liberal in posting vacation pictures and links to articles I've written, but I never mention how many of my pitches were rejected, or the times my husband and I argued about money or the messy state of our house.

I'm not particularly polished, but my feed is just as curated as any influencer's. I try to show the good, the bad, and the ugly, but when I feel hideous or have an ugly cry during an awful day, I don't rush online to document it. I may write about it later, but even then I know the experience is clouded by the whitewashing of hindsight. Nothing anyone puts into the world is entirely objective, and that includes the most authentic oversharers on the Internet. It definitely includes me. I'm not a manipulative person and I'm always going to tell the truth, but it's still just my version of a much bigger story.

Before I had kids, I was a compulsive reader of mommy blogs. I would read any half-interesting post I came across and kept up regularly with a few writers who frequently shared photos and personal stories with the world. As someone who looked forward to having kids and very much wanted to be a mother, I relished this glimpse into the future. It felt like a window into my own dreams and, in some ways, training for the years ahead. Through my favourite mommy bloggers, I learned about pregnancy, birth, and motherhood, and I grew to know the moms and their children as the months and years went on.

I stopped reading most of mommy blogs when I had children of my own. My desire to have kids had been replaced by actually having kids, rendering old windows into motherhood somewhat redundant—and I saw the blogs a little more clearly. I understood that I was only witnessing a tiny sliver of reality. I could surmise what wasn't being told and where the real stories were glossed over. I continued to read parenting articles and keep up with the blogging world, but I no longer clicked on the same three or four profiles regularly. I genuinely liked these women and enjoyed their voices, but once I'd experienced motherhood first-hand, I found the view far more expansive than anything I'd ever read. (Plus, I was very busy.)

I look at Instagram photos the way I look at ads in a magazine—I appreciate them as art, but I recognize how much direction went on behind the scenes. I know that each picture is selected for a reason and each caption is designed as a complementary message. The mom who wrinkles her nose in exaggerated dismay while showing off her messy kitchen in the background? Woman, you know you look cute with your face scrunched up like that, and your kitchen isn't even that bad. My kitchen is in *terrible* condition compared to yours, and I will never, ever offer photographic evidence to back that up. But I might like your photo anyway because I'm down to normalize messy kitchens and there's nothing wrong with having a cute face. Just do you, and I'll do me, and we can like each other's photos forever in this meaningless vacuum.

At one point, a friend mentioned she was struggling with how to announce her pregnancy. She seemed genuinely anxious about it: Should she post a photo of the ultrasound, a baby onesie with the due date in the caption, a cute maternity shot with her husband, something more creative? What were people doing these days? She was worried about not marking the occasion appropriately or, worse, posting something uninteresting.

I had no idea. I've seen all sorts of announcements online and they all seemed perfectly fine. I didn't announce either of my pregnancies—I just got pregnant and eventually people noticed. Sure, I told my immediate friends and family, but not with a carefully orchestrated announcement featuring a cute photo and a sweet caption. I didn't put a dinner roll in the oven so I could take a picture and make a pun or buy cute baby shoes so I could photograph them beside my own. As far as I recall, I felt no pressure to come up with a cute pregnancy reveal. Instead, I'd run into people and say, "Hey, by the way, we're going to have a baby." They'd congratulate me and ask the standard questions about due date and how I was feeling, and then we'd move on. This now feels antiquated in a world of Instagram photos, secret camera pregnancy announcements on YouTube, and elaborate gender reveals that result in forest fires.

Sometime in the recent past, expectations of women shifted to include public displays of motherhood. It's become standard to share everyday moments alongside milestone occasions. Special announcements are the new norm for a marriage, a baby, or a new job. It's cute if you enjoy the creative outlet, but it's just as acceptable to opt out, especially if watching everyone else's highlight reel makes you feel less good about yourself.

Of course, gawking at other parents' apparent online perfection is an offshoot of a more widespread digital envy. I am not a supermodel, nor am I a bridge troll. When I put on nice clothes, fix my hair, and do my makeup, I feel reasonably good about what I see. However, I spend ninety percent of the time with my still-damp hair in a messy bun, maybe wearing mascara. I work from home, so my daywear consists mostly of leggings and comfortable sweaters. My beauty routine could be described as "sporadic" and "practical." In the winter, I often leave the house in sweatpants because I'm convinced no one can see them under my winter coat, even though the coat only covers the top third of my legs. I'm extremely casual and I'm comfortable with that. But when I see the perfect skin, blown-out hair, and slim bodies of other moms on Instagram, I can't help but compare myself a little bit. I like how I am, but I'd love to have a thinner face and glowing complexion. Even when I see body-positive moms with their stretch marks on display, I think, *They're beautiful—mine are so much worse than that.* (They're not.)

I am fully capable of critical thinking around social media, and I know how warped it is, yet I still fall for the comparison trap. It's impossible to avoid, even as someone who is extremely media literate. I might know that I'm being sold a particular story or look, but I still internalize its messaging. I like my casual, somewhere-between-supermodel-and-bridge-troll self, but I would trade complexions or wardrobes with just about any influencer in a heartbeat. I want to wear the sweatpants but look really cute and pretty while doing so.

It's totally possible to love yourself and still hate yourself a little—or at least wish away your perceived flaws. It's not abnormal to have fluctuating self-esteem. But I know I wouldn't be thinking about these things as much if I didn't constantly have curated imagery to compare myself against.

Social media forces us to evaluate our parenting and our lives in ways we don't always recognize. When you see that incredible, Pinterest-worthy birthday party, you might feel guilty that you don't do that for your kids. The mom who shares adorable weekly or monthly photo updates of their new baby is way more organized than you are. The mom who posts pictures of nutritious, tasty school lunches in cute containers totally has her shit together. I mean, I'm that lunch box mom—I make really good lunches and I feel good about it—but I definitely don't have my shit together, and I don't judge your Lunchables. I have a million parenting weaknesses to make up for my excellent lunch box game.

It's so easy to get caught up in another person's highlight reel without stopping to consider the ways in which they might be struggling. I frequently assume that everyone else is doing great where I'm failing, and I'm way too hard on myself. But I know I'm a good mom. I'm aware of my failings, and also my strengths. I know how well my kids are loved. I also know there's no way to show that in any kind of post, and an infinite number of likes can't validate my parenting. I know what's real. My true highlight reel happens in secret, in the moments that no one else can see. Tucking my kids into bed at night, reading stories, and whispering to each other as we cuddle. My children are what's real in the world, and they are why nothing else matters—not even other people's immaculate living rooms or my own beautiful bento box lunches. Which is as good a reason as any for me to try to stop judging myself.

THE ART OF BEATING KIDS AT BOARD GAMES

My son, a six-year-old boy in a dinosaur T-shirt, sits across from me in front of an old chessboard that once belonged to his great-grandfather. He's holding a plastic knight in his little hand, humming quietly to himself as he debates his next move with the intensity of a chess master in his prime. His sister watches carefully, leaning over the worn grey ottoman that serves as our game table. She's going to play the winner, so she wants to know what she's up against. As with any serious chess match, an episode of *Wild Kratts* plays on a nearby television.

My son turns his head toward the television and then back again. "Did you know that hippos can't really swim?" he offers casually. The knight moves, and he takes one of my pieces. Dammit. And wait, how is that possible about hippos? How long can they hold their breath, and what happens when they sink? Are hippo drownings an issue I've never known about? Our game carries on, neck and neck, the Kratt brothers continuing their impossible adventure in the background.

When I play a board game with my children, I want to win. It doesn't matter if it's cards or Monopoly or the children's version of Settlers of Catan—I'll happily destroy them. I did not go through pregnancy and birth two humans just so I could pretend to be bad at chess. I mean, I'm not particularly good at chess either, but I'm still going to try my best.

When we play games that require reading, do I have an unfair advantage based on thirty-plus years of literacy that predates their existence? Sure, but that's not my fault. If they fumble over "counterclockwise" in an instructional card, it should motivate them to work on reading better. That's life, baby.

This isn't always true, of course—I do help them sound out words because I'm not that mean—but also, I'm not entirely joking. If they make a bad move, I let them make it. I'll explain the rules of the game clearly, but if they fall into a trap because they weren't paying attention, so be it—better luck next time. I love a good board game and I love my kids, and I respect them too much to treat them like delicate flowers who will wilt in the face of defeat. I'm playing to win, and they're doing the same. Failure has an important role in childhood development and building resilience. When I take them down in Clue, I'm teaching them that it takes practice and effort to succeed. Also, I'm showing them that Mommy excels at murder-themed games.

This isn't just my competitive streak in action—I also need to engage fully rather than watering myself down in the name of being a mom. If I sit there with my kids, letting them beat me at checkers again and again just so they feel good about themselves, I'm doing them no favours. I'm not doing myself any favours in that scenario either. I'd be performing a routine, one where I'm a playmate, not a whole person. A prop rather than a human being with motivation and skills. I'd be bored.

This is the sort of mom confession I fear getting skewered over, but it's true: many day-to-day moments in parenting are dull. Like sitting through a children's movie or making school lunches, imaginative play is something I do with my kids, but I'm not excited about it. It's an act of love. So when they pick the family edition of Trivial Pursuit out of the games cupboard and ask me to play? Hell yes, I'll play. I will play my heart out. I'll offer a loving mix of trash talk and encouragement. I might give a few hints or pointers if asked, but otherwise I'm on a mission to gently and lovingly take them down.

My son makes his bishop do a little dance, commenting on how many of my pawns he's taken. I move my rook and exact my revenge. "Dammit!" my child mutters under his breath. Because he is six years old, I remind him not to curse, but I'm secretly amused. It was an appropriate use of the word, and the aw-shucks vibe of the more child-friendly "darn it" doesn't have the same feel. We eye each other's pieces, trying to anticipate next moves. His sister has wandered off to find a snack.

I love these times with my children, casually sprawled around the ottoman in the living room. We laugh, we get mildly frustrated when the game isn't going our way, we chirp each other and have fun. The competition is real, but each battle ends with a friendly "good game"—and then my children immediately request one more round. This is how we manage the after-school lull or find quiet moments on a lazy Sunday afternoon. It's close to paradise.

(For the record: Chutes and Ladders is not a game. It's a curse. It requires zero skill and unlimited patience and is the coin toss of board games—ability has no value and there is literally no way to be either good or bad at the game, because it exists only as a meaningless time suck. If Hell exists, it is a fiery loop of Chutes and Ladders, endlessly shuffling pieces around the board according to a roll of the dice. There is nothing worse than Chutes and Ladders. Put that on my grave.)

So much of my life is spent with my children, nurturing their interests and abilities. I happily bake with them, sit and draw pictures, take them hiking, show them how to pick herbs or plant flowers in the garden, play tetherball in the backyard, or I read them endless stories. I sing songs at bedtime and dance in the kitchen. I'm a parent who spends quality time with her children, but I'm no good at playing dolls or pretending to be a pirate. I lack the ability to get lost in any imaginative game in which I have to be a character or, even worse, an animal. If you hand me a toy figurine, I will hold it with the awkward charm of a man buying a box of tampons for his wife.

Games, however, are where I feel at ease. They differ from other types of play-based interaction because they're a dedicated task for my brain, complemented by pleasant conversation with my children. Board games are a magical respite for someone like me who feels deadened by pretending to be a horse. They're a language I feel comfortable in. I can sip a coffee while I look my kid in the eye, capture his player with no remorse, then watch him jump up in glee when he figures out a countermove. High fives all around.

That said, the only thing that outweighs my desire to win is my pride in having happy, smart, capable children. Despite my very real attempts to kick their asses in a variety of skill-based board games, I'm thrilled when they do beat me. It's no different than seeing your kid fare well on their report card or score a goal in soccer—they're succeeding, and it feels good. It may not be a milestone you note in a baby book, but when your children beat you and your partner in Pictionary for the first or the fiftieth time, it feels like you've done something right. It's alarming how much joy they emit when they sink my battleship, but that's fine. The feeling is mutual.

There are so many ways to love your children—as many ways as there are to play. For years, I felt guilty about being the type of parent who begrudgingly gave horsey rides and was always quick to suggest that Daddy does them better. I didn't give myself nearly enough credit for all the love and attention I gave to my kids because I felt so bad about the handful of things I wasn't good at or didn't do. Some families bond over sports or Lego while others play backgammon. The love comes through, no matter what your quality time looks like—even if it's a semi-intense game of chess.

My son usually takes the win these days. He's mastered the art of playing well while half-watching a cartoon. He'll hover a hand over his king, his eyes wandering toward the television screen as he spouts a random biology fact. The more he does this, the more distracted I get, and yet he always seems to be two moves ahead. "Got you, Mama," he'll say triumphantly, slamming his player down as he closes in on my king. "I got you so good. Can we play again?"

We eventually run out of time, with dinners and homework and bedtimes always on the horizon, but tomorrow, or the day after, my answer is always yes.

SOMETHING TERRIBLE IS GOING TO HAPPEN TO YOUR FAMILY

The second I became a mother, I knew something terrible was going to happen to my family. I felt it in my bones—my children would get hurt or go missing, probably because I let go of their hands in a parking lot or let my eyes wander for a few moments at the park. I worried I'd be killed in a tragic accident, leaving them to be raised alone by their father, a wonderful and loving man who cannot cook and has never once clipped their nails or taken them for a haircut. I feared something would happen to my husband. This didn't feel like unrealistic apprehension but like fact, and I knew I had to remain alive and well until my kids were at least eighteen. More so, I had to keep them safe, but oh, how it seemed the world was against me—or, at the very least, my mind was.

A few days after I brought my first child home from the hospital, the nightmares started. I'd be calm and happy all day and then *boom*, disjointed sleep and ridiculous, horrible dreams that felt incredibly real all night long. They were wildly different from night to night but shared a common theme—a looming threat of harm to my newborn daughter—and they elicited an intense, overwhelming physical response. I'd wake up thrashing the sheets, convinced my baby had suffocated in bed next to me while I slept. She was always safely nestled in her bassinet. I dreamt a man on the subway grabbed her and I wasn't able to reach her before he ran off the train, the doors sharply closing behind him, the train speeding me away from her toward the next stop. Another night, I woke up soaked in sweat, an agonizing scream bursting from my throat as I tried to yell out to my mother, who in my dream had taken my infant on a roller coaster that was slowly ascending a steep, high track in preparation for the first big drop. They weren't even strapped in. I was in tears. None of it was real, but it felt vaguely familiar. Anxiety wasn't a new friend; it was just hanging out a lot more all of a sudden.

My brain has always been a strange place. When I was eight years old, I had a recurring nightmare that Queen Elizabeth II came to my home town and took a liking to my dog, so she claimed her as her own and took her back to England. Yes, this is what I most feared as a child, even as my parents were angrily divorcing and famine dominated the world news. I loved my tiny dog and was certain a powerful royal figure would steal her, given the chance. My logic was that the queen gets what she wants, and I assumed she'd totally want my dog if they ever crossed paths. This nightmare was genuinely upsetting and replayed for several years. I told no one, knowing even as a child that it would sound ridiculous if I shared it out loud.

My mind has always worked overtime to convince me that everything I love is transitory and destined to slip between my fingers. This dread applies to many areas of my life, but none so much as my family and my home. There is no fight or flight in my world; I'm one hundred percent fight, all the time. Consequently, I'm continually poised to battle anything that endangers the people I love. This mindset creates an exhausting tension that runs a current through everything I do, from maintaining my relationships and career to my sleep habits. It ebbs and flows in intensity, but it's never not there.

My mom was a single mother of three who, at one point, commuted ninety minutes each way to work. She used to leave around six-thirty, before my brother and sister and I woke up for the day; a neighbour would ring our doorbell an hour later to make sure we got up and went to school. We insisted our mom go into each of our rooms and say goodbye every morning, which meant nudging us partially awake, giving us a kiss, and saying, "I love you," before she left the house. She did this most days, but every once in a while, she was running late and simply left. On those mornings, when I woke up to a motherless home, I was devastated. Surely something terrible would happen to my mom that day and I'd never see her again, all because she hadn't said a proper goodbye. I often envisioned a car accident on the highway, we children only learning of it hours later, having waited alone in our townhouse as darkness fell. In those days, hardly anyone carried a cellphone. My mom had one—a massive beige brick like Zack Morris's phone in *Saved by the Bell*— but it wasn't always plugged in (it barely had a battery) and you couldn't hear very well on it. Thus, I often couldn't reach her, so of course I'd assume she was dead. These scenarios unfolded in my mind as I brushed my teeth before school, eyeing myself grimly in the mirror. As the oldest, I'd have to raise my siblings alone, I surmised. I could cook and run the house, more or less, but where would we get money for bills? At least I'd be able to drive in a few years.

"Your mom just went to work," a neighbour consoled me one morning on the walk to school, staring in confusion at my tear-streaked face. "Why is it so upsetting when she doesn't say goodbye before she leaves? It's the crack of dawn, she's tired."

I was aghast. "Because she might never come back."

The neighbour wasn't sure how to respond, and that evening our tired mom came home to my rage about being abandoned. She didn't understand my anxiety, and I didn't understand what it was like to be a thirty-four-year-old divorced woman with three children in a variety of questionable emotional states. In hindsight, it was a great dynamic.

People talk about mental health more than they used to, but I'm not sure how much this shift actually helps people like me—an anxious kid who turned into a super-anxious teen and remains a moderately anxious adult. I'm also unsure how much it helps mothers who suffer from more serious anxiety than I do. Talking openly about anxiety has benefits and helps minimize the stigma, but it doesn't make anxiety go away. Standard parenthood is ripe with worry, but this is more than that. A typical mother worries about bad things happening. An anxious mother waits for them to happen as if they're inevitable and lives according to this fear.

I was this mother. Looking back, I wasn't just an anxious person who became a mom—the problem was bigger and had a stronger hold on me. What I experienced went well beyond my usual quirkiness, but it was something I wouldn't identify as potentially harmful until much later. "Everyone gets the baby blues," people say, but I wasn't blue. I was genuinely happy, if also a little fucked up.

I'd heard of postpartum depression but not postpartum anxiety. I don't remember reading about it in any pregnancy books or hearing about it from my doctor or my friends. In fact, I didn't recognize how badly I'd experienced postpartum anxiety until years later. I assumed my standard-issue anxiety had peaked post-baby, probably due to a lack of sleep. I was a weirdo being extra weird because I was tired, and that was fine. So many things can be chalked up to "just being who you are," and this was a prime example. This wasn't a medical problem—this was my personality and, therefore, something I must endure—and hide, to an extent, so people wouldn't think I was a psychopath or question my ability to raise a baby.

I mean, I was so happy. My baby was wonderful. I wasn't stressed out at all by transitioning to life with a newborn. So why was I having horrific nightmares, and why did it feel like I was choking if someone took my baby into the next room, out of my sight?

Baby-wearing is a great way to hide separation anxiety, I discovered, and exclusively breastfeeding makes it easy to keep your child close at all times without seeming totally unhinged. That wasn't the reason I breastfed or bought an infant wrap, but it was an added bonus, so I ran with it. As long as she was with me, we'd both be fine. I didn't leave the house without her. I wasn't isolated—we went out to play groups, to the park, to run errands, or simply to walk around the city—but I never left her behind, not even when my husband was around, and I easily could have. It felt totally normal and, truth be told, I was content to live like that—until I woke up in a cold sweat, shaking from a dream in which my baby was switched with another child at the doctor's office and no one believed me. "This is your baby," the nurse insisted, holding out a strange infant while I kicked down doors, looking for my real daughter. Lying awake in bed, I forced myself to breathe deeply until my heart rate slowed to a normal pace.

I cannot stress enough how content I was during this time—a truth that sounds ridiculous, given what I was going through. It was a genuine joy to have an incredible child who smiled, laughed, cooed, and snuggled through her days. Mothering her felt like a natural extension of myself, and I loved being a mom; in every way that matters, I was good at it. My days weren't stressful in the least, and I almost felt like I was cheating motherhood by having it so easy. Until night fell, of course, and I turned into a shivering mess of feelings and bad dreams.

It got better eventually, but just better enough. While the dreams faded over the course of a few weeks, my anxiety held tight in other ways. I'd bought concert tickets when I was pregnant, but as the date approached, I eyed my four-month-old child and knew I wouldn't go. The thought of leaving the house without her for a few hours was overwhelming. I blamed my absence on her inability to take a bottle—I'd honestly tried to get her to accept one, in an attempt to share feeding duties and get more sleep at night—but really, there was no way I would have gone. I gave the ticket to a friend and stopped making plans that weren't infant-friendly.

Many iterations of my anxiety have appeared over the years, and even now, with my kids somewhat older, I still battle a more manageable physical response to being separated from them. Their first days of school were an emotional disaster for me (I cried in my car; the kids thrived). I felt like throwing up the first time I sent them on a bus to summer camp, knowing they'd be off in the woods for eight hours before I could see them again (naturally, the kids loved camp). No matter how hard it was, I kept sending them out into the world. My instinct is to helicopter, but I've made a point to fight this urge, steeling myself against the stress I've come to expect and giving them space to explore. I don't actually want to home-school them or keep them in a bubble—I just don't like how it feels to leave them with strangers in a strange place.

You might think I'm entirely risk averse when it comes to my children, but that isn't true. I very much want them to take risks—to put themselves out there and try, and fail, and push themselves to do better. I'm even okay with a reasonable level of physical risk—but only if I'm there. I might let them climb a super-tall tree at the park or scale the frame of a play structure while I stand nearby, but I don't want them to walk to school alone. I'm not so afraid of kidnappers, but the idea of them crossing the road unsupervised makes me feel ill. This logic may be flawed, but it's how I function.

If I were to list the things that cause me genuine anxiety today, it would include busy public spaces where I might lose track of my kids, people other than myself or my husband taking my kids pretty much anywhere, play dates and/or birthday parties that I don't stay at, summer camp (especially ones with swimming), the possibility of my children choking on grapes, anything to do with water or moving vehicles, and school field trips. I see the potential for very bad things everywhere, and I subsequently freak out in my head on a near-daily basis. I refuse to cross the street unless we are at a crosswalk, and even then I make intense eye contact with drivers to make sure they see us. I don't drive on the highway; when my husband does, I clench the armrest. If he speeds on a rainy day or stops the car too close to train tracks, I will yell at him for putting our lives in danger. I am a pleasure to be married to.

Anxiety is a motherfucker, and I cannot shake it. Nor do I always try. In many ways, I feel like these stresses keep my family safe—like if I somehow lost all sense of tension and foreboding, the worst would happen because I'd no longer be on guard. My complacency would be the death of us all. And so, I let my anxiety live a little—it may be exhausting, but surely it serves an important function. Right?

I hide all of these feelings from my kids—or at least I try to—and that alone is a big job. I'm pretty good at it most of the time, or people let me think I am anyway. Many people consider me a relatively chill person, though notably, those people aren't my husband, immediate family, or close friends, who know better.

I don't want to pass my anxiety on to my kids. Part of this is out of my control—genetics, the things I'm unable to hide, pure luck—but part of it feels like an undertaking I can handle. If I keep my anxious thoughts in my head, my kids won't hear them. If I maintain outward calm and composure, they won't pick up on how tense I am. If I let them go on that play date or field trip, they won't know I hate everything about sending them off to a place that's not my house, with people who aren't me. When they go outside and play with their friends unsupervised, they don't need to know how often I spy on them through the window. They get their freedom and I slowly adapt to their expanding world. I take deep breaths and hide the parts of myself that don't function optimally, trying to prevent my kids from inheriting that which I don't want to share. I'm doing what I can to shape their futures into ones different than my own.

It's exhausting, this way of parenting. It often feels like I'm navigating Pac-Man World instead of real life, but I know I'm far from alone. And if I get a little better at this parenting-through-anxiety thing each year—even the tiniest, smallest, most incrementally teeny bit better—we'll get by. Even if I'm faking it.

INTERLUDES IN MY DRIVEWAY

I am a mom who sits alone in her car for five or ten minutes before going into the house. This is not so much an escape as it is an interlude: a quiet, interim moment between one task and another. It's a pause, an opportunity to recalibrate before I join my family inside. My brain operates both too fast and too slow, and sometimes it needs to be reset before I change gears.

So I sit in my car for a little while, doing nothing at all, which feels nice.

This doesn't happen every time I leave the house, of course—there is often dinner, bath time, bedtime, or some other immediate responsibility to attend to. Or there might be groceries in the trunk that need to be packed into the freezer before they thaw. I'm not always able to steal time for myself. But when no one is waiting for me, I sit alone in my car. I finish my thoughts, soak in the silence and stillness of my driveway. I might check my email or scroll through Instagram or stare out at our front garden, which always needs weeding, but most times I just let my mind drift. It doesn't matter what I think about. An interlude is whatever you need it to be.

I am an extrovert who loves being around friends and family; I'm a physically affectionate person who needs conversation and touch. I am also someone who craves solitude and regularly seeks it out wherever I can get it. This doesn't always mean hours of time and space to myself; that's not usually attainable, especially on demand. Sometimes six or seven minutes in a vehicle that's not moving on my own property, meandering around in my own head, has to be enough.

There's something lovely and rebellious about sitting in place, not doing anything, however briefly. Motherhood does not always allow for this. That's why I make it happen, sneaking in moments that are both selfish and self-preserving.

I am a mom who goes out for a drive at the end of a long day, heading no place in particular but always taking the same lakeside route around the bay. I turn up the radio as the road disappears beneath my wheels, singing along to old songs, taking in the final streaks of sunlight on the horizon. The road winds over hills and through a small, forested area sprinkled with stately brick houses and spacious modern builds, many of which sit on the grave of a torn-down century home. Timed sprinklers bathe the lawns of the wealthy, giving the street a glossy sheen as my headlights move through the falling night. My car groans as I crest each hill, its aging engine making itself unapologetically known as I cruise neighbourhoods. I cross the yellow line as needed, giving ample space to late-night joggers and old men in plaid pyjama pants walking their dogs. I watch for wildlife along the road, often spotting coyotes, red foxes, or families of raccoons.

When I'm feeling especially restless, I go for long evening walks, my dated headphones plugged into an iPod Classic, even though yes, I know a phone can hold songs now. I don't care. I plug my corded headphones into my music player and stride purposefully down the streets, wondering if the people I pass can hear the music blasting from my ears. My playlist is full of pleasures I no longer feel guilty about. I gaze into strangers' houses from the sidewalk, their insides aglow with soft light, and tell myself this is an act of aesthetic admiration and therefore isn't creepy. (It's a bit creepy.) I walk past gardens and note the absence of weeds. It's funny how two people can plant the same array of lavender, irises, and delphinium and deliver such different presentations. I wonder if a homeowner is retired, or hires a gardener, or is simply less lazy than I am on weekends.

I am a mom who for years could barely find the time to shower, but who now takes long, hot baths at the end of a long day. Tucked below my bathroom sink is a stash of cheap, spa-inspired face masks from the drugstore that feel luxurious but are probably terrible for my skin. I put them on with the same naive enthusiasm every time, then wonder later why I'm breaking out. In the bedroom, I've slowly built a stack of unread books, a personal library that always offers something new and exciting to delve into as I soak in flower-scented, pink-tinged waters. When a book is good, I lie underwater until my skin is thick with wrinkles; other times I abandon it beside the tub in favour of shut-eye and the hum of the overheard fan.

And sometimes, when I'm so tired that even a bath feels like too much work, I curl up under a blanket on the couch and read until my eyes burn. Just one more chapter, one more page, one more sentence. I read until the words blur and my mind closes the door to comprehension. That's when I get up, drink a glass of water, and turn off the lights, then slide into bed beside my responsible, disciplined, long-asleep husband. I could go to bed earlier, but when else would I find the quiet I crave? Sleep isn't the same as rest. I need both.

I am a mom who has created a series of moments out of instinct and necessity. I know the value of each and every interlude, even when they take me away from other tasks or leave me tired because I've traded sleep for peace. I know what these moments fix and what they don't. They aren't equal to a good night's rest or a more manageable schedule, but they recharge me in small but helpful ways. They are a bridge that carries me over and through. This is what I can do, and what I will continue to do until I no longer need to.

I am a mom who sits quietly in her car—just for a moment—before she dives back into the world.

THE THING YOU LOVE MOST ISN'T ALWAYS FUN

My daughter was born on a cold, snowy February night. The first six months of her life happened mostly during spring and summer, blissfully warm, outdoor months that led to many long walks and afternoons spent at the park. Sometimes those sunny afternoons were all about her entertainment, and I'd spread out a soft flannel blanket and a few items to keep her busy: a stuffed bunny, a board book, a set of plastic keys. We'd share a handful of Cheerios and watch squirrels tear across the park, their deft but harried bodies narrowly escaping the neighbourhood dogs. My daughter would roll off the blanket and tear handfuls of grass from the ground, marvelling at her own strength. She didn't have many toys, because we hadn't thought to buy them, but she loved to watch an endless stream of water pour from the massive, pitcher-shaped fountain in the green space between two nearby apartment complexes.

Other times, visits to the park were decidedly for my own enjoyment. With my child safely and contentedly strapped into her stroller, I felt no guilt about letting my mind wander as we walked. Some days I'd skip the park altogether and just stroll, grabbing a coffee and meandering around our neighbourhood as my daughter cooed at people and animals. We'd head south along the smoother parts of Philosopher's Walk at the University of Toronto, just ten minutes from our apartment and perfect for idling along in good weather. If you happened to be in the right place at the right time, classical music would float out through the open windows of the Royal Conservatory as rehearsals took place within. I'd find a bench or a flat rock and sit for a while, nursing my daughter as students, musicians, and tourists walked by.

Once she was satisfied and sleepy, I'd settle her back into the stroller and start again, this time with the seat reclined and the sunshade pulled all the way down. Once she was deeply asleep, I'd find a shady spot under a tree in the park and sit beside the stroller, reading whatever beat-up novel I'd stashed in my purse. If it was late enough in the day, we'd meet my husband at the subway and walk home together, our little family of three happily reunited.

Each and every stage of motherhood has been sprinkled with moments of joy, mostly everyday things that warm my heart with simple pleasure. The wonder and excitement of first words, first steps. The first lick of a slice of lemon, reacting to the sour taste and then trying it again. Watching my toddler carefully pet a neighbour's dog. The sound of giggles under a blanket during a game of hide-and-seek. The feel of my child's arms wrapped tightly around my neck as I carry them into the house after they've fallen asleep in the car. Watching my kids devour ice cream cones on a hot summer day. Their spontaneous hugs where they clutch each other tightly and fall to the ground, laughing.

These moments are my favourite thing in the world, and in them I recognize that I'm a capable mother raising two awesome, loving human beings. This is wholly, irrevocably true. And I am being equally truthful when I feel like a complete failure who shouldn't be allowed to be in charge of plants, let alone human children.

A different scene: my infant son screaming, which wasn't unusual in the first year of his life. The house nearly vibrated with his wails. My daughter, who typically accepted her afternoon nap without hesitation, was also inconsolable, overtired, and in desperate need of sleep. They were keeping each other awake, the thin wall that separated their bedrooms doing nothing to stop the noise. Instead of wearing themselves out, they seemed to be readying for battle. I moved between the two rooms, soothing and rubbing backs. After what felt like hours—but what was probably more like thirty minutes—I was also in tears, mentally exhausted at having failed miserably to soothe either one of them. We all needed naps. I also needed a shower and a proper meal. Instead, I sat down in the dark hallway and put my head in my hands, the wails of a baby-and-toddler death metal concert reverberating through both the house and my brain.

Hours later, my husband came home, tired from a long day at work and a long commute. "How was your day?" we asked each other mechanically, both of us replying, "Fine." Technically, we could catch up later, but by the time both kids were in bed and the kitchen was cleaned up for the night, neither of us would feel like rehashing the worst parts of the day. Venting often felt pointless or selfish because I know we would have gladly traded places for twenty-four hours—I needed a break from domestic life and missing the part of my brain that came alive when I worked outside the house, and he was tired of the banalities of the corporate world and wished he was home with his kids.

What we both needed was balance, which is always harder to obtain than it should be. To parent is to be pulled in all directions at once, and more often than not, it's doing what benefits your kids, because that's the promise you made when you brought them into this world. Not that this stops you from quietly wondering if you've pushed yourself too far down on your own to-do list.

Parenting is often enacted out of love rather than enjoyment. It can be tedious, frustrating, and absolutely exhausting. This may seem obvious, but it's rarely said openly and without guilt. Not loving parenting is not the same thing as not loving your kids. You can love your children more than anything in the world and still get bored when there are three more hours until bedtime and you've already used every trick in the book to fill the day. You can love your kids and be annoyed when they whine, irritated when they don't listen, or resentful that your partner still has a career and social life while you're a twenty-four-hour milk bar. I love my kids so much that I miss them when they're sleeping—and yet I don't enjoy every moment they're awake. This has always been true. It's also totally normal and okay.

My daughter was a year and a half old when my son was born, which essentially meant I was parenting two babies at once. One, a tiny newborn with lungs designed for all-day screaming, and another who could run around independently and offer opinions, even though she was still in diapers. They rarely, if ever, napped on the same schedule. If one slept through the night, the other did not. Sometimes they both wanted to be held at the same time, so I'd park one child on each shoulder, murmuring words of affection into each ear and making sure they both felt secure and loved. I usually managed to keep everyone calm and happy, but when I couldn't, it felt like time stood still and I was trapped in a vortex of crying. I didn't go into motherhood expecting it to be easy, but I hadn't anticipated the doubt and guilt that roared out of feeling inadequate on those hard days. My empathy for my children was endless, but in the early years of motherhood, I struggled to afford myself that same compassion and care. Instead, I beat myself up for everything I thought I did wrong and didn't give myself nearly enough credit for all the things I did right.

I remember holding each of my babies in my arms when they were still newborns, believing they were absolutely perfect and knowing I'd do anything for them. They'd cry and I'd gently rock and sing to them with all the patience in the world. After all, babies fuss and toddlers have meltdowns—it's what they do. "It's hard to be so little and have such big feelings," I'd tell them, wiping away their tears. "Mama knows it's hard. It's okay."

If you told me that one day I'd give those same sweet babies the finger behind their backs because they wouldn't stop arguing about who was the rightful owner of a particular stick in the backyard, I wouldn't have believed you. I hadn't snapped after countless sleepless nights, tantrums, and fits of colic, so I probably never would, I reasoned.

I was wrong—my patience does have a breaking point. I've stormed out of a room to give myself a time-out. I've hissed threats at my children in the car as they fought like cats in the back seat. I've used my outdoor voice in indoor settings. I start most days with patience, but sometimes it runs out before bedtime.

I've never once felt good about any of this. But my deepest shame? That sometimes, during those long stretches of weekday afternoons in the first few years of motherhood, I was bored.

This revelation came to me when my kids were toddlers, and it took me by surprise. I don't know if it was their age or my complicated relationship to the suburbs, where we'd moved when my youngest was still an infant, but every afternoon felt a hundred years long. Of all the challenges of motherhood, I didn't see this one coming. I've been peed on more times than I can count, had my sleep disrupted for years, and cleaned poop off the wall of my bedroom at three in the morning because it shot out of my newborn like a cannon, and none of that shocked me in the least. I felt ready to give myself to my kids, even if that meant giving up parts of myself (temporarily). I'd put my career dreams and social life on hold in order to be their mom first. But I didn't anticipate having to endure a persistent sense of boredom, one that made me wonder if there was something faulty in my maternal makeup.

If you've ever spent time with a toddler, you know that children themselves are rarely boring. How could anyone so energetic, impulsive, and full of wonder be a bore? My kids aren't boring, and I love hanging out with them. The older they've grown, the more this is true. But those early years when I spent hours at home in a never-ending pattern of play, feed, sleep, repeat? It bred a certain monotony that no one would describe as exciting. I loved reading to my children, but doing it for hours on end, day after day, made me start to mentally check out after a few stories. I could read a book aloud while thinking about something else entirely, my mind stretching beyond the confines of the eleventh rendition of *Moo Baa La La La*. Did this make me a genius or a terrible mother? I'll never know. I've considered both possibilities.

I was also unprepared for the times I became downright annoyed with my children. The little things always drove me mad—they still do. Years after growing out of obnoxious toddler moves like throwing sippy cups or soaking an entire room with water at bath time, they've grown into new habits that make me want to pull my hair out. My daughter sits with her legs on either side of her chair at the dinner table, like she's riding a horse, and for some reason this irritates me to no end. "Please sit properly," I repeat every night. Then her brother absent-mindedly starts to hum the *Jurassic Park* theme song for the millionth time, and though he's remarkably on key, the sound is like nails on a chalkboard to me. *I could do without this*, I think to myself. *I could go for just one family meal without a dinosaur song.*

Is it weird that I never really considered that my kids would sometimes annoy me? Even the most wonderful people are insufferable on occasion, me included. It makes no sense that my children would be exempt. Did I think I could love anyone so much that they'd never irritate me? *Bad mom!* a voice whispers despite all logic, but I am not. I have come to believe that if a particular person has never annoyed you, you probably don't know them intimately enough.

Who hasn't counted down the minutes until their partner arrives home, so they can get just a moment alone after a long day of tending to their child's every need? Who hasn't longed for the opportunity to hear your own thoughts as you think them, or to maybe pee (or even shower!) uninterrupted? God forbid you linger at the grocery store for longer than necessary or stop to get coffee on the way home to buy yourself an extra ten minutes of quiet. None of those things make you a bad person. They announce a desire for basic self-care.

Afternoons are different now that my kids are older. I don't have babies anymore, or even toddlers—I have school-aged children who yell, "I'm going out!" on a Saturday afternoon and then disappear with the slam of a front door, happily running off to meet up with their friends. *Stay here and hang out with me*, I want to tell them, overwhelmed with more freedom than I can bear. I putter around my office or the garden, wondering how I keep ending up with free time. And then I waste it, because I've grown unaccustomed to having any.

When the kids are in school during the week, I often watch the clock, daydreaming about what they're doing and how their day is going. I hope their classmates are being nice to them and that they're having fun while they learn. Instead of counting the minutes until their father gets home from work to give me a tiny break from parenting, I count the minutes until I get them back from their teachers. I still find new moments of everyday happiness that flood my heart with love. I still lose my patience in the car or at the dinner table. We love each other. We annoy each other. It's still not always fun, but it's what I signed up for when I became a parent.

"You'll miss this one day," people say to moms who are in the thick of the hardest years, but they're wrong. I don't miss running between two bedrooms while my babies scream endlessly, or cleaning poop off the wall in the middle of the night. I didn't finally start sleeping through the night again just to wish I could sleep less, like I did in those new-born days. I've never yearned to go back in time, no matter how much I love that new-baby smell. I look back on those idyllic afternoons in the park with nostalgia but know that my same happiness exists today, albeit in different moments with the children those babies have become. I don't miss the hard parts—at least, not yet. But I don't regret them either, not for a second. Everything you love is worth putting work into. Parenting is work, but it's worth it. Especially because you always remember the sweetest parts first.

I WANT TO BE A PARK DAD

Moms have fantasies all the damn time. The sweetest of dreams, the dirtiest of secrets, and everything in between—our yearnings are buried deep inside, quietly burning to be fulfilled.

One of my greatest fantasies is to spend a single day being treated with as much respect as a man who adequately parents his children in public.

Picture him: some guy taking his kids to the park, just a regular parent doing regular parenting things. Not any man in particular—the everyman, with his own children—but a *man* and thereby incredible and exceedingly good. He doesn't need to be doing anything extraordinary—pushing a stroller or carrying a diaper bag is enough. But if he plays catch or pushes a swing? Best dad ever. So hands-on! So doting, so involved! It's spectacular to witness a man like that in action. He is clearly a gift to his family; his wife is so lucky. Don't you think?

I want to be him, the park dad, in all his mediocre glory.

There are park dads outside the park too. A man who drops his kids off at school in the morning is a treasure. A dad at the doctor's office, volunteering for a field trip, or taking part in a parent-tot dance class is a goddamned hero. A man who can brush his daughter's hair and put it in a ponytail? Basically a god.

A man in public with his children is deemed worthy of respect and admiration simply because he is there. He is fawned over for doing the bare minimum—loosely supervising his own offspring in a public space—and every move he makes is gold. He brought full water bottles? Amazing. Is that sunscreen? Yup, what a responsible father. Snacks? Of course he brought snacks, what a guy. Aww, his kid's shoes are on the wrong feet—how cute!

A mom at the park is completely unremarkable. Mothers are everywhere—the library, the grocery store, the park, all over the place—and no one blinks an eye. Unless her children act out, of course; people are very quick to notice when that happens. We do everything with offspring in tow, so much so that our children feel like an extension of our own bodies. Most moms can carry a toddler and three bags of groceries into the house in one trip, unlocking the door with one hand while balancing the rest without a second thought. Their children cling to them in their beds after a nightmare, talk to them while they shower, and ask questions while they use the toilet. They're in our laps, on our legs, and wrapped around our necks—sometimes quite blissfully, other times despite our desire to (gently) shake them off. Especially in those early months, our children are literally attached to our bodies for much of the day.

I remember attending a baby shower when my daughter was two or three months old, a tiny kitten of a child I'd dressed in a soft but impractical lilac dress. I spent much of the party pleasantly chatting with friends and acquaintances, gently bouncing my daughter in my arms as I spoke. I conversed while bobbing up and down, patting her back as needed, rocking her as she slept briefly, pausing only to nurse her in an empty bedroom. Finally, a friend's mother approached me with a knowing smile.

"Go get something to eat," she said. "I'll hold the baby."

I thanked her, realizing how hungry I was, and gently placed my baby in her arms. Grabbing a plate, I chose a few things from the buffet and joined some friends standing in the kitchen. I could see my daughter across the room, content and half-asleep in a room full of strangers, not the slightest bit concerned that she'd just met the woman who was holding her. As much as I was happy to snuggle my baby all day long, it felt good to have use of my hands for a few minutes while enjoying a meal among other adults.

It took about five minutes for me to realize that I was still gently bouncing up and down, moving my feet in the same perfect rhythm that always soothed my baby, in the same careful motion I repeated for hours each day, moving around the house with my child in my arms or bound to me in a stretchy fabric wrap. I'd handed over my baby, but my brain had not, and there I was, mindlessly comforting a plate of pasta salad, rocking my lunch to sleep.

Wonderful as he is, I don't think my husband ever had the same experience. Sure, he loved our baby more than words could say, but I'm pretty sure he didn't feel like he was missing a limb when they were apart. He still went to work and ate meals alone and used the washroom without considering what that meant for supervising our child. When he showered, he was just showering—not calculating how long he had until the next feed or positioning the stream of water to help relieve clogged milk ducts.

I had to consciously stop behaving like my child was on my body because she almost always was. This wasn't a problem—this emotional and physical connection was a joy, most of the time—but the weight of that responsibility was heavy and impossible to walk away from. I couldn't just eat a sandwich. I had to tell my body to consciously stop repeating the soothing motion my child demanded, that it was okay to rest.

I'm not remarkable in this regard. A lot of moms will read this and think, *Yes, this was me too.* They made dinner while nursing in an infant sling or sang songs from the washroom in order to calm a fussy baby while they showered or peed. They remember how it felt stranger to be without their child attached to them for a moment than it did to have a second human layer. To be everything to a tiny person, via labour that is not only expected but also invisible to the rest of the world.

This is what moms do. We don't do it for recognition or glory; we do it out of love. For many of us, this attachment feels normal—so wonderfully, awfully normal—and for long stretches of time, we don't give it a second thought. And on the other hand, there are the park dads—doing things every mom has done a million times but revered for the labour. And we notice.

It's not the park dads' fault, honestly, and no one should be mad at them. Most of them are probably excellent fathers. I'm sure many of them have rocked babies for hours themselves or made dinner with a child latched around their leg. But they've also benefited from the ridiculously low bar set for men who attend to their children. A mom has to be perfect to be good. A dad just has to be seen to be perfect. That's not fair to anyone.

I dream about being a park dad so I can do the things I already do and also finally earn society's nod of approval. Hell, I'd settle for ambivalence—because while everything a mother does in public is judged, a father is treated as extraordinary for doing literally anything. If you've ever heard someone talk about how a guy is so "hands-on" because he changes his own child's diapers, you know this to be true. Imagine the reaction to a mother who *didn't* change diapers? The horror.

Here's how my fantasy goes: In my alternate life as a dad, I get to the park dressed in comfortable sweatpants and a loose T-shirt. Nobody thinks I'm lazy or a slob; they view me as relaxed and practical. My kids run ahead of me, practically vibrating with energy, and strangers smile my way—how wonderfully active those young ones are! I sip from an enormous cup of coffee, stifling a yawn. He must have been up with the little one in the night, the other park-goers whisper among themselves, and yet he's still here at the park when he could have put on a movie instead! What a good man.

One of the kids wants to be pushed on the swings, and I oblige. A nearby grandmother swoons, surprised by my involvement. When my older child falls and scrapes a knee, I comfort them, clean the area with a baby wipe, and quickly apply a bandage. The other parents admire my empathy and skill. "Don't feel bad," someone says. "Kids fall all the time. It can't be helped." It's nice to be reassured that this, like so many other things, isn't my fault.

Snack time! The kids are hungry, so I get out water bottles and granola bars, or maybe apple slices. Noting the sun, I spritz sunscreen on my children's pale legs as they eat. Another swooning grandmother gasps at my preparedness. "Where is your wife?" she asks gingerly. I reply that she's at work, and the entire park falls deeply in love with me at once. "Well, you're doing a wonderful job," the grandmother assures me, speaking for everyone. "She's a lucky woman to have you! You're obviously an amazing father." I smile and thank her for the compliment.

After an hour or so, I give the kids a five-minute warning: "It's almost lunchtime!" One of the park moms asks what's for lunch, and I tell them it's boxed macaroni. They laugh. Don't all kids love boxed macaroni? Everyone does. What a treat. You do the grocery shopping too? My goodness, aren't you a catch.

I mention a parent council meeting I'll be attending next week, and they practically fall over in excitement.

One of the kids wails as we head home, causing a bit of a scene, but it's okay. After a few minutes of fruitless negotiation, I tuck my child under my arm like a football. Nobody judges my parenting style; in fact, several observers chuckle affectionately while offering words of support. "He's so patient," someone whispers. As we walk past them to the sidewalk, I joke that nap time can't come soon enough. "Have yourself a rest while they do, Dad," they encourage warmly. "You've earned it!"

Pushing the stroller home, I'm greeted with looks of admiration. "It's great to see a dad like that," someone observes as we pass. "Out here on his own with his kids. Look how cute he is with that diaper bag!"

I am awash in the glow of collective approval for doing the very same things every mom does. I have parented in public, and for that I am now saintly. My status in the neighbourhood is forever golden. I am, by all accounts, a Good Dad. I managed the basic elements of child care without the accompaniment of a female parent. It feels nice. I think?

Except maybe it doesn't. I don't know what it's like to live on the other side, but I imagine this gets old really fast. I know many great dads who would agree—being endlessly patronized isn't a compliment. They don't need praise for parenting their own kids. They don't even want it. Because as much as it can sting to be underappreciated, no one wants to be treated like an anomaly.

Perhaps this is my real fantasy: We normalize dads taking on more and recognize more of what moms do every day. We accept that parenting is beautiful and joyful and hard, and that a trip to the park doesn't illustrate the sum of any parent's role. We recognize that not every family is a 1950s nuclear model and shift our baseline accordingly. Or maybe, just maybe, we treat *all* parents the way we treat that regular dad we see at the park.

MY FERAL CHILD, MY LOVE

My son is perched at the top of a climbing structure at school, casually holding himself in place with one hand while the other stretches out loosely in the breeze, pointing vaguely to something in the distance. He doesn't sit on the web of climbing rope, as the structure intended, but at the very highest point of the metal frame. He looks happy and peaceful as he surveys the world around him, oblivious to the stress he's causing some of the parents below. Not me—I'm used to the sight of him balancing perilously high above the other children, his forty-five-pound frame braced against the wind—but a few of the other moms don't know him and look seriously worried. They glance around, wondering where the hell his parents are. I offer a friendly wave, indicating I'm aware he's up there.

"He's a bit of a monkey," I say as I walk over, smiling awkwardly and hoping they aren't judging me too harshly. Sometimes other parents will respond with awed laughter, other times pained silence. Occasionally, they wonder aloud if he should be up there at all, or what would happen if he were to fall. "He'd probably get hurt," I admit. "But he's a very good climber, and I generally don't stop him unless it's been raining or something." Allowing him to sit at the top of a slippery metal climber is my limit—I do have one.

Eventually he makes his way down, gracefully leaping to the ground from the halfway point. "Did you see how high I was, Mama?" he asks excitedly, as if I might not have noticed him four metres in the air, waving his arms like a bird about to take flight.

"Yup," I reply. "You were pretty high up there! Were you being careful?" He laughs and shoots me an amused glance.

"It's not hard," he insists. "I'm careful but I'm a really good climber. Aren't I, Mama?" He runs off before I can answer. The other moms look relieved to see him on solid ground.

As a child, he started doing planks at five months old, straightening himself into a push-up and staying there, seemingly impressed by his own strength. He was crawling at six months, walking by nine months, and running soon after. If you've never seen a ten-month-old baby, lean and small for their age, who can somehow stand up unaided and bolt across a room, allow me to confirm: it's terrifying. It's like watching a doll come to life in that it seems completely unnatural, but that was my son. A tiny hurricane of energy, running under tables and climbing everything in sight.

I don't think nature ever intended a one-year-old to have the agility of a kindergartner and the vocabulary of a drunk college student, and yet he is real, he is mine, and I love him like crazy.

My son is as brilliant and wild as they come. He made this clear the day he was born, when he came out screaming and didn't stop for fifteen minutes. I rocked him as best I could in my hospital bed, baffled by the intensity of his wails. Why was he so mad? He had just been born. How had I offended him so immediately, and why weren't my snuggles and coos enough to calm him like they'd calmed his older sister? Staring into his bright red face, I immediately knew this child would be nothing like his sibling.

In some ways, this boy is extremely civilized. He will discuss science at length, using all of the proper terminology and even throwing in the occasional Latin name (a habit that tends to both impress and confuse those around him). He requests salmon and asparagus for dinner, and steals sips of my lattes, insisting that coffee is his favourite drink (he's never had more than a tablespoon or so at a time, but he loves the idea of coffee as much as I do). His brain never stops, insisting that he soak in every how, why, when, and where. He asks big questions and has big feelings. And without fail, he makes those feelings known.

When he learns a few mild swear words, he starts using them frequently and accurately. He doesn't know the F-word yet but he's proficient in his use of "what the hell" and "dammit," which amuses his father and I and dismays the grandparents. We talk a lot about context. He continues to mutter these words under his breath, louder when he's mad. In other moments, he explains bioluminescence with startling accuracy. One day, he confidently tells our seventy-five-year-old neighbour to stop letting his garbage blow all over our yard. I shout an apology over my shoulder as I hurry us back into the house, embarrassed by the interaction. I scold him, though he's not wrong—they keep their recycling bin outside on their porch, and yes, the contents regularly blow into our yard. "It's bad for the environment," my son notes. I sigh because he's right, it is.

The boy is affectionate in every way, throwing himself into hugs and curling up against me in bed when he's had a bad dream. He snuggles up when we read stories, twisting my hair around his finger until it's tangled in a knot. He tells me he loves me and that I'm the best mom ever—no other mom is better than me. He means this, even if it's not true.

One day, the school calls to say he's gotten in a fight with a boy several years older than him. It's not the first time I receive a call like this, nor will it be the last. After school, I ask him what happened. "He said my name in a mean way and called me a dumb little kid," he says, pouting.

I ask what happened next, and he's unapologetic. "He pushed me and then walked away, so I jumped on his back and made him fall over. I am *not* a dumb little kid!"

I do not approve, but the other boy doesn't bother him anymore.

Though he is agile and exceedingly capable for his age, he also runs into hard surfaces headfirst on a regular basis.

At age one, he flew face-first into the track that holds up a sliding glass door, slicing open his forehead. Naturally, he did this while I was out getting a massage—the first one I'd gotten since my children were born.

"I don't think it needs stitches," my mother-in-law told me when I got home, her voice revealing a limited degree of confidence behind this statement.

I peeled back the Band-Aid my husband had applied and found an open wound staring back at me. "I'll take him to the hospital," I replied. He received three stitches and a lollipop.

At age two, he climbed out of his crib and wandered into our room, tugging on the comforter to let me know he was awake. "Let's get you back to bed," I mumbled groggily, and off he went, happily running back to his crib in the dark. It would have been fine if he hadn't tripped on the carpet and fallen into the corner of his wooden toy box, slicing a deep, jagged gash through his eyebrow. Scooping him into my arms, I felt the blood before I could turn on the lights to see it. We went back to the emergency room for another set of stitches.

A few years passed before he needed stitches again—this time at age six, because he exited a room rather dramatically, smashing his face into a metal plate on the door frame as he spun around indignantly. More stitches, again on his face. Having now achieved a hat trick, I'm not eager to explain a fourth set of facial stitches to a doctor, and to be honest, he's running out of pristine face to scar.

When climbing trees, his movements confident and deft, he shouts animal facts down at me with zero context. "Did you know that sifaka lemurs are immune to the poison in trees where they live? They live in Madagascar! And they can avoid dangerous tree spikes because they're very good jumpers. They jump like *this*!"

Other times, he'll hand me a clover, his mouth full of green leaves. "They taste like green apple. We learned this at camp. They're not deadly. A lot of wild mushrooms are though. You never eat *those*."

This child can name the dinosaurs and sharks with ease but never remembers to brush his teeth. He rarely wears a coat unless I make him, and he doesn't like boots because it's easier to climb trees in running shoes. He sings along to the radio without a care in the world. He's barefoot whenever possible, and when he sees a bug, he picks it up and gently carries it back outside. One summer day at the cottage, we hear the distinctive sound of a rattlesnake before spotting it on the path ahead. "Is it a massasauga or a diamondback?" he asks, trying to get a better look. "Get inside—it's poisonous!" my mother quickly advises. My son is unfazed. "Grammie, rattlesnakes aren't poisonous. They're venomous." Quietly, we watch it slip back into the woods.

Some will say this is life with a boy, but I don't think gender has much to do with it. He's a sweet little wild thing who seems to have a bit of wolf cub or baby bear in him despite his suburban upbringing. I'm sure he has contemporaries somewhere, but I've yet to find them. Nature seemed to correctly guess that only one child of his ferocity would fit into a single family.

I wouldn't change a thing about my son. He is not something to be altered or moulded; he is utterly, wholly himself in every way. We parent the children we get, no matter who they turn out to be, no matter how hard we try to convince ourselves we have any control in the matter. Nurture is important, but nature is ever powerful. I can love and guide my son through life, but in the end he is who he was always meant to be: brilliant, exhausting, loving, hilarious, and wonderfully, perfectly mine.

ZOMBIE RATS

My husband and I bought a house in the suburbs for two reasons: a lack of access to the ridiculous wealth needed to buy a house in Toronto, and our aversion to the mice slowly taking over our rental unit. Mice, we came to realize, are hard to get rid of—particularly when you're busy parenting an infant and a toddler, you haven't slept more than three solid hours in a row in months, and your landlord thinks you're exaggerating the problem. (We were not.) We could have found another rental in the city, but prices were sky-high, and we figured that if we were going to move again—for the third time in three years—it might as well be into something we owned. My husband craved housing security and a yard, and I couldn't justify anything else.

So off to the suburbs we went, where our money got us a four-bedroom house with a monthly mortgage payment that was significantly lower than the rent for our two-bedroom apartment. Sure, I didn't want to leave the city and had put off our inevitable move for months, but the mice finally won. I was done sharing my home with tiny, sneaky creatures that chewed their way through our belongings, pooped in our dining room, and explored my children's toy box at night. Animals don't usually make me squeamish, but living with mice is where I drew a line. My kids deserved better, and my husband and I couldn't stand our rodent roommates any longer.

Our new house was simple but spacious and had a good-sized backyard. We moved in late winter, and as spring-time slowly turned everything from grey to green, we began spending more and more time outside. I planted a stupid number of hydrangeas and raspberry bushes, then added an herb garden packed with basil, dill, and lemon thyme. My father-in-law bought the kids a swing set, and we found one of those little plastic cottages to complete their play zone. I was having a hard time adjusting to the suburbs, and the backyard was a welcome reprieve from my stress; it was a safe, peaceful place where my kids could run around for hours at a time. It was the first part of the house that felt like it could be home.

And then one day, while looking out the kitchen window, I saw a large, rodent-like creature wander out from behind our shed and into the garden, pausing beneath the bird feeder to collect fallen seeds. It was brown with a long tail and a fat, wobbly body. I watched it for a few minutes, trying to determine what it was. It was far too large to be a mouse, but too small to be a groundhog, and not weird enough to be a mole. Was this a vole? I'd never actually seen a vole, but it seemed plausible. I made it as far as googling "vole" before I was distracted by something my kids were doing. In any case, I wasn't too concerned.

I saw the little guy again a week later. And then again—but this time, he was with a friend. Two small brown animals with rotund bellies and slim, slithery tails. I was nervous: what were these things? Memories of the mouse-infested apartment filled my mind, but I tried to remain calm. It was probably a harmless suburban garden animal I'd never heard of. People would laugh it off when I told them. This whole thing was silly and not really a problem. Everything was fine. Until a visiting friend happened to also see our portly garden pests returned to pilfer seeds again. "Holy shit, Erin," my friend said in alarm. "Those are rats."

Of course they were rats.

We determined they were coming from under our shed. They likely had a burrow there, which explained why I often saw them sprinting back in that direction with mouths full of seeds. We removed the bird feeder, but the rats soon took up another home—in my herb garden, which they tunnelled into, traipsing through my bountiful parsley like rodent kings. I cried, devastated that my suburban paradise was just as pest-filled as our downtown rental had been. The only saving grace was that this time the rodents were outside, not in.

I'd like to say we used humane ways to trap the rats and free them in a nice meadow by a stream, but I won't lie to you. After trying many, many non-lethal methods to get rid of our former apartment mice, we were well past that idea. My husband put out a series of snap traps.

"Do you think that will get rid of them?" I asked, huddled under a blanket on the couch. No sooner had I spoken those words than we heard a snap through the screen door. After a moment of silence, we heard another.

We killed two rats immediately. They were small—not the bigger ones I had often seen gathering seeds—which confirmed there were definitely more than two living under the shed. The logical part of my brain had always known there were likely more than we'd seen, but the assassination of two rats in under a minute was a bit unnerving. My husband threw out the bodies, reset the traps, and came back inside. We killed another four rats before morning. It was horrifying.

And so developed our new suburban evening routine: set the backyard traps, go to bed, lie there staring at the ceiling, wondering how many rats we'd have to kill in total to solve this problem. My husband set his morning alarm fifteen minutes earlier than usual, so he'd have time to remove the bodies before the kids and I got up for the day.

Now, you might think I wouldn't set foot in the backyard while all of this rodent murder was happening, given how disgusted I was by the whole situation. But we weren't really seeing the rats anymore—if we hadn't been catching so many at night, I'd swear there wasn't a rat problem at all. Because there were few parks within walking distance and we had a baby who still napped twice a day, I sometimes took my three-year-old daughter outside to play on her swing set or kick around a soccer ball. My husband had talked me into believing this was okay, since the rats weren't nearly as bold as they had been. "We've probably got most of them at this point," he insisted. "Just take her outside." And so I did, though reluctantly and never in sandals.

This is how I happened to be standing in the grass on a sunny afternoon, watching my toddler happily amble around our yard, when I witnessed the most disturbing rodent-related sight to date: a fat brown rat stumbling toward my daughter in a slow daze, like a rodent zombie. I screamed and scooped my daughter up, nearly falling over backward to get away from the rat while trying to keep an eye on it. It continued to wander aimlessly through the grass, noticeably unsteady on its feet. I took my daughter inside and went back out alone to investigate.

The rat was bleeding profusely from a serious head injury. It was stumbling around not because it was sick or lazy or just plain bold, but because it was dying. It had been caught in a snap trap and was terribly wounded but not killed. I felt awful. I had done this to the rat, by proxy. He was my responsibility now.

I sat on the back steps and called my brother in a panic. "What do I do?" I asked desperately.

He took a deep breath. "Do you have a shovel?"

"Yes," I answered slowly.

"Okay. Do you think you could smash the rat with the shovel?"

"No. Absolutely not."

"I knew you were going to say that," my brother conceded. "But you need to put it out of its misery."

"I can't kill an animal," I pleaded.

"You basically did though," he said. He wasn't wrong. Still, I knew there was no way I'd be able to end its life, even if I was the one who'd gotten it into this mess. I called my husband.

"Just leave it out there and it'll die in peace," he said. "Maybe it will wander back under the shed and die there."

"IT'S NOT PEACEFUL," I shouted. "IT'S A ZOMBIE RAT AND I WANT IT GONE."

He sighed, asking me what I wanted him to do while he was an hour away at work.

"None of you guys are any help!" I cried, heading back into the house. My daughter peered out quizzically from the living room where she was watching cartoons. "Everything's okay, sweetie!" I called. Everything was not okay. None of this was okay.

I don't remember making any decisions about what to do next, but I did something: I grabbed a large Tupperware container meant for keeping cereal fresh, and then I grabbed a red broom. Armed with these household objects, I found the rat—still stumbling around, its head still bloody and gaping—and I placed the Tupperware a few inches in front of it, the pour-hole wide open. Taking a deep breath, I grabbed the broom and lined it up behind the rat, in line with the Tupperware. And then, with the precision of a champion mini-putter, I tapped that rat into the plastic container.

And then I screamed, because now that I had it contained, what the hell was I going to do with it?

I took a photo of the rat in the Tupperware and texted it to my husband and my brother, who were impressed and puzzled and unable to help me. It began to sink in that I really, really didn't have a plan. And then it hit me—I would call animal control.

A woman answered after a few rings and asked what the nature of my call was. I cleared my throat anxiously. "I have an injured animal."

"Is it a dog, a cat? A wild animal?"

"It's a wild animal."

"Ma'am, what type of wild animal is it?"

"It's a—rat, I think. It's an injured rat. I found it in my backyard." I coughed, deliberately omitting the specific context of the rat's injury. The woman seemed surprised but remained professional. "We'll send someone over shortly."

And they did. The animal control van showed up within half an hour, the staff in full creature-catcher outfits and everything. I took them into the backyard and showed them the Tupperware. They stared in confusion and asked me what had happened.

"His head is sort of crushed...becauseoftherattrapsinthebackyard." I mumbled the last part with an apologetic shrug. Fortunately, the animal control people seemed more amused than angry.

"We're going to take him, and we'll put him down," one of them said. "But you cannot half-kill a rat in a trap and then call us to take it away. You need to call an actual exterminator. Can you promise me you'll do that?"

I promised, and they began to walk away. I shook with relief. It was over, sort of. We still had rats in the backyard—I was more certain of this than ever—but the zombie rat was gone, and it'd be dead soon, humanely euthanized to make up for a horrific, inhumane incident with our snap trap.

"Hey, ma'am?" The animal control person was calling me from the driveway. "Do you want your Tupperware back?"

I politely declined and went into my house to call an exterminator who, as it turned out, was really great at his job. The rats were gone within a few weeks, and we never saw evidence of them again. Apparently, poisoning animals is the best way to kill them. If there's one thing my life in the suburbs has taught me, it's that you don't want to half-kill an animal. No, ma'am, you want to fully kill it and its whole family for $350 plus tax, like a real grown-ass homeowner. And that is what I was—a grown-ass homeowner with a backyard, a rat-free shed, and one cereal container short of a full Tupperware set.

THE SLOW AND TRAGIC
DEATH OF SANTA CLAUS

Tiptoeing into my daughter's bedroom in the middle of the night, I stop to listen for the sound of slow, deep breathing that tells me she's truly asleep. I hear the thick hum of children dreaming and carefully move forward. There are toys everywhere, piles of books beside the bed. Our cat stares at me in confusion and I will him not to move, lest he wake the child he's curled up beside.

There's a subtle shift in position from the small frame on the bed, and I drop silently to my knees. The stillness quickly returns, but I know my time may be short. More panicked than I should ever be in my own home, I quickly place a chocolate bunny at the foot of her bed and leave a trail of Easter eggs back to the door, practically flying back into the hallway. *Fuck yeah, I did it!* Now I have to successfully repeat the same mission in my son's room. Only then will I go to sleep—victorious, but also worried the treats will attract bugs in the night.

Just another night as Mom, the keeper of magical lies.

I am of two hearts about the mythical beings of childhood. There's nothing like seeing your kids' faces light up with joy at the sight of the Easter Bunny's chocolate eggs or presents from Santa. A visit from the Tooth Fairy brings them far more pleasure than it should, given the terrifying concept of a small winged creature making off with teeth in the middle of the night. My own childhood memories are tied up in these moments—Easter egg hunts, digging into a stocking on Christmas morning, coins under my pillow where a tooth used to be—and I've done my best to create those memories for my own kids. I want them to feel the same thrilling anticipation when they know magic is near, however strange or unbelievable it might be, willing themselves to fall asleep so they can wake up to something extraordinary.

So I put in the work to make holidays special for my family. I've carried on my family's traditions and helped create our own. I've snuck into dark rooms more times than I can count, snatched teeth from under pillows, baked cookies with overtired children on Christmas Eve, chewed on carrots left for reindeer, forged letters from St. Nick, and feigned surprise when my children delightedly told me about these things the next morning.

I'm also over it. I'm more or less ready for my kids to figure out that, much like the Great and Powerful Oz, holiday magic is just me creating illusions from behind a curtain. I may be a fraudster, but I'm one with good intentions.

I've never told my kids that Santa is real. I've certainly implied it—particularly when I leave special gifts under the tree and sign them *Love, Santa*—but I've never flatout argued on behalf of his existence. Between school, commercials, pop culture, and grandparents, they've been thoroughly sold on the existence of the jolly giftgiver. I just haven't done anything to make them believe otherwise. And when they ask questions? I become a master avoider. I gaslight the hell out of my children about Christmas, and I will continue to do so until they force me to answer with a simple yes or no.

"Mama," my younger child has asked me. "Is Santa real?"

"Hmmm," I reply seriously. "What makes you ask?"

"Because there's no way Santa can get all the way around the world in one night, and he always leaves exactly what we want, every year. And reindeer can't actually fly."

"Those are interesting points," I concede. "What do you think?"

"Well, I think it's you, because we tell Santa what we want, and he gets it. But also, the stockings. The stockings always have our *favourite* stuff, and we've never asked Santa for any of that. He wouldn't know. But you know."

"I do know what you like," I admit. "But part of the magic of Christmas is believing."

"Do you believe in Santa?" my son asks.

I hesitate, then answer slowly. "I believe in the magic of Christmas, and maybe part of that means choosing to believe in Santa. Not thinking about logic or what makes sense, and just believing in the spirit of Christmas. So in that sense, I choose to believe."

"But you're the one that brings the presents and does the stockings probably," my son begins, then changes course optimistically. "Or maybe you tell Santa what we like?"

"Anything is possible," I say with a shrug. "You can choose to believe whatever you want to. Do you want to believe in Santa?"

"Yeah, but I think it's you."

"Well, maybe just enjoy Christmas then and try not to worry so much."

He's satisfied with this for now, and exudes happiness on Christmas Day.

My older child is either a hard-core believer or a really good faker. Likely it's a bit of both: she wants to believe in Santa Claus and the Easter Bunny so badly that she convinces herself they're real, no matter the evidence. When her brother questions the existence of Santa's elves, she is horrified. She tells me about the kids in her class who don't believe and seems incredulous, but other times she gives me a wink that suggests she knows more than she lets on. Shortly before Easter one year, she casually mentioned how much she liked those chocolate carrots the Easter Bunny had brought last year. Then, looking me dead in the eye: "It would be really great if we got those again this year. You know?"

I laughed, raising an eyebrow. "Suggestion noted."

She nodded back with a smirk. "Thanks, Mama."

Easter came around, and she was thrilled when the bunny came through. "He got our favourite kind of chocolates!" she squealed happily. "The Easter Bunny came!" For a moment, I wasn't sure what our earlier conversation had meant. Did I imagine she'd asked me for the chocolate carrots, knowing the Easter Bunny was me? Did I misinterpret her intent? Maybe she simply thought I'd tell the Easter Bunny somehow?

But then, a little while later: "Mama, we can't find the last few eggs." (The Easter Bunny had left instructions that included the exact number of eggs to find, because I didn't want to find melted chocolate under a couch cushion sometime in June.)

"Oh?" I asked, unsure of what she wanted from me. "So… keep looking, I guess?"

"Mama," she whispered intently. "We need a hint."

"Ohhhh," I replied. "Look higher up? Check the walls."

"Thanks!" she chirped, bouncing away. Moments later, as she collected chocolate eggs from the top of a picture frame, she called out again. "Got 'em! Thanks!"

I still don't know what any of this means, but a child who pretends to believe is all the fun with much less pressure—so, if anything, I'm in the golden age of holiday parenting.

The Tooth Fairy is another story entirely. What may be a charming ritual in other households is decidedly darker in ours, and that's all my fault. This is because the responsibilities of the Tooth Fairy are sporadic and somewhat stressful, and I find the whole thing creepy and gross. I hate loose teeth, I hate sneaking teeth out from under pillows, and I never carry cash. Teeth fall out whenever they happen to fall out, whether I've got the right change in my wallet or not. Sometimes I leave a two-dollar coin, other times it's a pile of nickels and quarters or even an IOU (sorry, kids). Everything about the Tooth Fairy is a pain in the ass.

I have collected teeth and flushed them down the toilet so my kids won't spot them in the trash. I have also collected them and, in the foggy-headedness of exhaustion, left them on a table in our front hallway where my kids found them the next day. "Mama, my tooth is here!" my daughter cried out one morning.

"Oh, no," I replied in a half-conscious daze. "That's a tooth from my childhood. Grandma kept it for thirty years and then got it out to show me when I told her you lost a tooth. Isn't that gross?"

I changed the subject, asking what she wanted for breakfast and hoping there were no follow-up questions or future interrogations of Grandma, who would either fold or tell a more elaborate lie to cover up my ineptitude. Neither outcome was ideal. Again: the Tooth Fairy is the worst.

Or maybe I'm the worst.

When my children's suspicions about the validity of the Tooth Fairy first arose, they decided to leave her a note. Like most people, they wanted to know what her deal was with collecting baby teeth.

Dear Tooth Fairy: What do you do with the teeth? the note read in messy, poorly spelled children's printing. They left the note beside my daughter's bed, where we'd gently placed a baggie holding one of her incisors. Both kids went to bed with great anticipation of the response to come. For reasons I can't fully explain or defend, the Tooth Fairy's return message was as follows:

I eat them.

Did this answer freak out my kids? A little. When the next tooth was lost, they left another note.

Dear Tooth Fairy: What do the teeth taste like? (A strange question, given that the teeth had lived inside the letter-writer's mouth for over six years.)

Dear child: the small teeth are salty, and the molars are very sweet. Yum!

In the morning, my daughter was satisfied by the discovery of two dollars under her pillow but disgusted by the information on the note. "Ugh, I can't believe she eats our teeth," she said, her nose scrunched up in mild horror.

Her brother joined in, perplexed. "Why would she do that?"

"You bite your fingernails," I pointed out. "I've seen you eat them."

"I don't eat other people's fingernails," he retorted. Fair enough.

If Santa Claus and the Easter Bunny are magical elements of childhood, the Tooth Fairy is their obnoxious cousin who keeps showing up uninvited. I'm ready for her to fly off and never return, but she isn't taking the hint. And for some reason, my kids still buy it—either that or they want the money and will pretend to believe in a magic tooth collector forever to get it. That's the problem with smart kids who have big imaginations—they may be legitimately invested in the idea of a fairy who eats their teeth, or they're quietly extorting me. Who's to tell? I may never know.

I enable my children's belief in our magical visitors because I'm not entirely ready for those chapters to close. One day my kids will casually hand me their Christmas lists instead of shyly whispering things to a man with a beard who's dressed head to toe in red. There will be no more annual photos with Santa, and I won't have to wait until they're asleep to put presents under the tree or gnaw on carrots they've left out for the reindeer. When this happens, I'll feel relief as well as genuine loss. There's a reason I still sneak into their rooms so carefully. I'm fine with them figuring out the truth, but I don't want it to happen because I tripped over a plastic dinosaur and awkwardly ruined the magic. Let it be gentle, gradual.

At times though, I want to tell them what goes on behind the scenes so they don't become the weird kid in

Grade 7 who still believes in Santa. Is it my job to make sure the truth does come out? I've concluded that some kids stop believing in incremental steps. First, they realize their parents are Santa, the Easter Bunny, or the Tooth Fairy. They live with that knowledge but pretend not to know. They continue to enjoy the myth, refuse to admit anything out loud, and maybe even appreciate that their parents keep up the charade for their enjoyment. They cling to these last pieces of magic, playing along for their parents' sake as well as their own. And slowly, quietly, they let us know they're in on the secret—maybe with a wink and a nudge, or maybe in actual words—and then, with any luck, they continue to play along.

My daughter finally showed her cards one evening after dinner. Her brother had just lost a tooth and I'd quietly made a comment to my husband that the Tooth Fairy had better find a toonie by the time our son woke up in the morning. Our daughter raised an eyebrow and sidled up beside me, looking around to make sure her brother couldn't overhear. "I have some toonies in my piggy bank," she whispered conspiratorially. "You can borrow one. You know, to be the Tooth Fairy later."

I nodded, surprised and relieved by her assistance. "I'll pay you back," I replied in a hush. She smiled and quickly ran up to her room, sliding a coin into my pocket when she returned. Crisis averted.

In the morning, she cheered in delight as her brother announced the Tooth Fairy had come. "Yay!" she cried out with a big smile, seeming genuinely pleased. My son ran out of the room, treasure in hand, and she glanced at me knowingly.

It's sad, the slow goodbye to childhood magic, but it's necessary. We can appreciate the years spent with Santa and the Easter Bunny, both as kids and again as adults, and then mourn the end of an era that gave our lives a little sparkle.

What a gift it is to relive these traditions through your children's eyes, to be a part of the magic again.

I meant what I said to my son about choosing to believe in holiday magic—we might know the truth, but that doesn't mean we have to stop believing. We can choose to surprise one another with a perfect stocking, or a favourite treat left at the foot of the bed. We can choose to believe in something that brings us joy, however complicated or illogical, and help keep it alive for those around us as an act of love. It's all love, in the end, and that's why I'll keep the magic alive for as long as my kids will let me.

THE SUBURBAN DREAM

When I lived in Toronto—the place I was born, where I'd hoped to raise my kids and live the rest of my life—it felt unmistakably like home. The city was comfortable, not unlike a warm sweater or the arms of a loved one, and its familiarity made me feel safe and whole. The constant hum of city sounds is, for me, like a white noise machine that helps a baby sleep through the night. I enjoyed nothing more than stepping outside my door and getting sucked into a cloud of sound and action. I felt no draw to subdivisions; I just wanted a room of my own in a place I belonged.

My old neighbourhood is full of beautiful old brick houses with tiny front yards; tall, skinny, semi-detached dwellings; and sprawling single houses that have been converted to apartments or renovated into modern dream homes. There's a lively arts and music scene, and streets filled with people at all hours. I loved going out for a coffee and stumbling upon a random festival on Bloor Street or a pop-up gallery in a park. I loved the underfunded public transit system everyone hates (even though it is fairly awful) because its existence meant I didn't have to drive or even own a car. There was always plenty to do as a couple, with the kids, or by myself, from concerts and museums to checking out new parks or restaurants.

My career felt tied to living in the city, where everything happened, and I never felt a lack of opportunity or inspiration. My husband's office was close to where we lived, and we had everything we needed within a twenty-minute walk of our apartment. I adored city life. Except that living there meant renting an expensive, too-small unit in a triplex with an active mice problem. And that we'd likely be renters forever because the cost of real estate in Toronto is astronomical.

My husband and I had a decent household income. We paid off my student loan by living in a basement apartment and spending next to nothing for several years, but thanks to the high cost of living, we weren't exactly swimming in cash. Objectively speaking, we were of average financial means—not wealthy, but certainly not poor—while doing the best we could to save. Our goal was a house in the city: a tiny, run-down, semi-detached in a decent neighbourhood was more than enough for me. But it was a lofty dream, even with all our hard work and privilege.

We saved aggressively, amassing a fairly large sum of money over the course of several years, but realized it wasn't enough. Soon after our second child was born, a family member gifted us a generous sum of money with the condition it go toward a down payment on a home—an unexpected event that was as surreal as it was shocking to me—but even then, the only urban dwelling we could afford was a tiny condo with sky-high maintenance fees. I wanted to stay downtown, but it didn't make sense to raise a family in a mouse-ridden, shoebox-sized apartment or a condo we'd soon outgrow when we suddenly had enough money to buy a four-bedroom house in the suburbs.

Relenting to financial logic and my husband's desire for a yard, we gave our landlord notice. I started having panic attacks immediately, but it was too late. Two months later, we moved into a two-storey home with a spacious yard and a kitchen that more than one person could stand in. We had bought into the suburban dream.

Living in the suburbs still doesn't feel entirely real or permanent. I've always thought of this as a temporary chapter in our lives, and yet there are no real signs of us ever leaving. This is my life now. I am a thirty-five-year-old married suburban mother of two. I drive a gleaming white crossover with leather seats, have a large garden that I complain about weeding but take great pride in, and I've been co-chair of our parent council for several years. I am so fucking suburban. I hate everything about this identity and yet I'm not unhappy. I am, however, restless.

When we first moved to the suburbs, my anxiety skyrocketed. I'd wake up early every morning and lie in bed, listening to the birds outside my window and hating them fiercely. Our old bedroom faced a busy Toronto street, and I was used to the sound of cars, people, and sirens at any hour of the night. My new bedroom was silent; outside, there was nothing but empty sidewalks and an endless parade of boxed-in lawns. You could hear a pin drop. When the birds started chirping at dawn, I'd wake up confused, wondering where I was and what was happening. As reality set in, I'd clench my jaw and resolve just to get through another day. My husband, who now commuted over an hour each way to work, would leave before the kids woke up and return just in time for dinner. My hours in between were long and lonely.

I hated driving but knew I needed a car. I spent almost six months fighting this decision but soon realized the only thing worse than having to drive everywhere was not being able to drive anywhere. There was nothing within walking distance of our subdivision, aside from a small strip mall that housed a pharmacy, a bar, and a Highland dance studio. There was also an educational resource store, which I visited too often and spent too much money at because it was one of the few places I could go during the day. Beyond that, it was all houses, churches, and gas stations. I tried taking the bus with my infant and toddler strapped into a double stroller but found it unreliable—sometimes the route would change without notice, and other times the bus wouldn't come at all. When it did show up, the bus was usually empty, which explained why the schedule was so erratic—it didn't matter if the bus showed up on time because hardly anyone used it. At the best of times, the bus only appeared every thirty or sixty minutes and stopped nowhere near my house. The suburbs aren't designed for people without cars—you drive or you suffer. At least I had the means to choose. I thought about this a lot when I bought my first vehicle, a second-hand Mazda that had belonged to my sister. In a cruel twist of fate, she had just moved into our old Toronto neighbourhood and no longer needed it.

There were so many things I resented about my new life that it felt like I struggled to accept them on an hourly basis. I was also overcome with guilt about not feeling grateful enough for having what so many other people yearn for. I had a wonderful husband, two beautiful kids, and a home that was not only ours, but ours by way of a large financial gift. Sure, I worked hard, but I'd also been given a handout that made home ownership not only possible but relatively easy. The suburb we lived in was actually really nice; many people around the world live in truly dire circumstances, I reminded myself frequently, but I was somehow finding ways to be unhappy in Canada's number one mid-size city. When I couldn't get around without a car, I bought one. I worked casually from home, but my husband's salary was enough to cover our expenses. I'd struggled in many ways growing up, but now my life was easy. All I had to do was be a suburban mom. What did I have to complain about?

My grievances sounded ridiculous as soon as I tried to vocalize them to friends and family. It was too quiet. It was boring. It didn't feel like home. There never seemed to be other kids at the park. I didn't like having to drive everywhere. The streets were always empty, and everything closed at nine o'clock. I missed quirky independent shops and restaurants and hated all the big box stores. I wasn't sure how to build a career in the suburbs. I hated my husband's commute. A house was more work than an apartment, and I couldn't keep up, especially with two kids under three. Time and again, I was reminded of what I'd gained (a house) and told to stop thinking about what I'd lost (my home).

On top of all the things I actually hated was the overwhelming feeling that I'd had no choice in the matter. My husband hadn't pressured me into leaving the city, but I'd felt a heavy responsibility to make a decision that was good for my family. And I'd felt additional pressure to accept the incredible monetary gift that would provide the security my husband wanted.

At the time though, I was less than six months postpartum with our second child and probably shouldn't have been making life-altering decisions. My emotions were real and my struggle with the transition to the suburbs was valid, but I felt like a monster. When people asked how I was adjusting after the move, I'd shrug while deciding how honest to be.

"You'd rather be back in that tiny apartment with the mice?" someone asked, trying to convince me I didn't mean it when I said I was having a hard time.

"Well, no," I'd reply, because what mother wants their children living in a cramped apartment with rodents when they can give them a house and a yard? "But I miss living in the city," I'd add, because I did, desperately.

Every question felt like a test of my motherhood. "But the kids didn't even have their own bedrooms at your old place. Aren't you glad they have their own bedrooms?" Yes, but I don't think kids sharing a bedroom is a big problem either.

"The kids have a backyard now! Don't you love it?" Sure, but we had lovely city parks with actual people in them, and I liked that more.

"You're closer to family! Your mom lives just around the corner, right? That's so good for your kids." My mom worked full-time. In Toronto. We didn't see her any more than we had before the move.

"Kids need stability. It's better to own than to rent." Is it still better if you can barely get out of bed in the morning?

I hated myself for feeling the way I did. I wanted to adapt to the changes but didn't know how. Each week grew harder instead of easier, and the stress ate away at my soul. When I took the train back into the city to meet a friend for dinner a few months after the move, I half felt like I was going home, even though the city was a place my family no longer held space in. On the way back, I yearned for my apartment instead of running to catch a commuter train headed toward a house and life I didn't want. My husband was at a loss; he didn't want to move again, but he was growing just as unhappy as I was, stuck between his lengthy commute and sad, deeply resentful wife.

I fell into a deep depression. Admitting it felt spoiled and grossly privileged, so I buried myself in suburban life, trying to find my footing in a building I owned but didn't belong in. I forced myself to drive the car until it felt relatively normal. I decorated the house and planted flowers in the yard. I got a Costco card and signed my toddler up for soccer. I faked happiness for my kids, who deserved a happy mom, and simmered with rage at the thought of my husband sitting at his desk in the city, hardly ever with us in the home he'd wanted. My constant despair had ruined that first-house milestone in a lot of ways, and we'd both underestimated how badly his commute to work would affect our relationship and his ability to spend time with the kids.

"Is Daddy going to visit us today?" my toddler daughter asked me one afternoon.

"He'll be home for dinner. Is that what you mean?" I asked in return.

"He comes to our house for dinner," she responded matter-of-factly. I was confused for a moment, and then it dawned on me. Her father was gone before she woke up every day. When she came into our bedroom in the morning, I was the only one there. She saw him for maybe an hour before bed, and he was gone again when she woke up. He sometimes missed dinner and bedtime if a train ran late. Aside from weekends, she barely saw him. She wasn't quite three years old and had interpreted all of this to mean that we had moved to the suburbs without him.

"Do you know that Daddy lives here with us?" I asked carefully. "He sleeps here every night. He just leaves early for work. But this is his home."

She shrugged, not seeming to buy it. "Okay."

My heart broke for her and for my husband, who was crushed when I shared this with him. He had already started looking for a job closer to home, but it would be almost two years before he landed one. In the meantime, he was a weekend dad, and I was stranded in our miserable new world. Nothing felt right.

We signed my daughter up for preschool and I made some friends, which helped, but even in my happiest moments I was looking for an exit sign. I wanted out of my misery. I didn't have to thrive, I just needed to feel okay. I spent hours on real estate and apartment rental websites, wondering what would happen if I made arrangements to lease a new place in our old neighbourhood. I'd just do it, I thought. Surely my husband would follow me there. It would be the decisive jolt we all needed. I imagined selling the house and going back to our old life, falling back into the happiness we'd felt just months earlier. (I clearly had a selective memory about the mice.)

Deep down, I knew it wasn't that simple. We'd bought a house—a huge undertaking—and going back to renting would mean repaying the family member who'd helped with our down payment and losing everything we'd spent on moving costs and realtor fees. The rental market wasn't exactly friendly to families of four. I'd barely managed to secure our last apartment, as landlord after landlord hesitated to rent to a couple with a baby. ("She's small now but soon she'll be a toddler who runs around all day, bangs on the floors, and annoys the other tenants," one told me.) And to be honest, I was too depressed to make any more big life decisions.

I'd experienced periods of depression before and usually crawled out of it in good time. It wasn't pleasant, but there were typically specific reasons for my mental struggles, and I always expected to see the other side. But this was the first time I'd experienced depression as a mother. I had a baby, a toddler, an absent husband. My children depended on me for literally everything they needed. I couldn't sit with my grief or work through my feelings—there was no time. I mothered all day, collapsed from mental exhaustion every night, and then did it all over again and again.

A full year went by, and nothing improved. I still hated the suburbs and had grown to hate our house. My husband's commute was still brutal. I was still looking at housing websites on a weekly basis and would often send my husband real estate listings for houses on the outskirts of the city. "We could make this work and renovate it over time," I'd write hopefully, sending him pictures of a tear-down at the top of our budget with no electricity and raccoons living in it. He was always stricken by the huge price tags and the state of the houses, many of which appeared to be falling over and were nowhere near any of our preferred neighbourhoods. Desperation had clouded my judgment.

I had the idea that we could purchase something in the city with rental income potential—a basement apartment maybe, or an upstairs suite that could be rented out to students or a young couple. This quickly proved impossible— after all, we hadn't been able to buy a small house in the city on our first go, let alone one with an income suite—and I was back to square one. Somewhat more realistically, I started to wonder if my mom might want to share a house with us. She'd grown up in Toronto and still worked there. She hated her current commute and didn't love maintaining a house on her own. She loved spending time with her grandchildren, and my sister already lived in the city, so if we made the move, it would mean being close to two of her kids. I broached the idea, and my mom was open to it, given the right property. The problem was that even with a third adult on the mortgage, finding a house in a desirable neighbourhood with room for an in-law suite was nearly impossible on our budget.

The further away from our old life in the city we got, the more trapped I felt. Initially, the move had felt like something I could undo if I tried hard enough, but after well over a year, I was beginning to crumble. I had to make a dramatic change, but I didn't know what that meant or how I would do it. The kids were still young, and I was determined to fix things before they grew more aware of, and affected by, my mental state. This became my singular goal: to erase the damage we'd done to our lives.

And then an opportunity presented itself.

My aunt mentioned that her neighbour's house was for sale and had been sitting on the market for a while. She lived in the same suburb we'd already moved to, but closer to the lake, in a walkable area with shops, restaurants, parks, and, most importantly, some of the liveliness I was desperately missing. It wasn't Toronto, but it felt like a solid compromise: houses with yards but also places to go and a sense of community. The house sat on a spacious lot on a quiet court near a bike path, but it was only five minutes away from the lakefront and downtown. My aunt lived next door and it was walking distance from my grandparents' condo. The listing was above our budget ("What budget?" my husband might have said, not convinced we could afford to move at all), but it had a huge unfinished basement that would make a great in-law suite. My mom and I made an appointment to see the house together that afternoon.

We went over without my husband, who was at work and understandingly overwhelmed by my overnight transition from "wife who looks at MLS every night and cries" to "wife who is viewing an expensive suburban house with her mother and has serious intentions to buy it."

The house was perfect. Aesthetically, it needed a lot of work, but it had good bones. The backyard was huge. The top two levels were spacious and offered plenty of room for our family of four. The basement was a blank slate, so we could build something where every element was designed for our needs. My mom liked the idea of living next door to her sister, and I loved the downtown neighbourhood. I knew my husband would be charmed by the location too. There was an elementary school around the corner. I was sold. This would be our compromise house. This is how I would live in the suburbs without falling apart. This house would save me.

My mom was willing to give it a shot, partly because there would be far less maintenance and paperwork for her to deal with and she'd be surrounded by family. She also knew we couldn't afford the house without her. We called my husband, who was decidedly unconvinced but agreed to see it. It was expensive (but viable, with my mom on board). It was still the suburbs, so how was it going to be any different? (It felt different. It felt more like me.) What if we moved and I was still depressed? A house couldn't fix that. (It would fix the source of my depression, I promised. It would pull me out of the quicksand I'd been living in for eighteen months. I just knew.) It was a huge leap with no guarantees. My husband saw more risk than benefit.

I continued feeling selfish and ungrateful for putting my family through so much. I missed a life that had made me happy but hadn't worked for my family. We owned a house many people would kill for but I didn't want. I was actively trying to buy a more expensive house to "compromise."

The term "First World problems" came to mind frequently. This felt like the most selfish depression of all time.

But that house on the court quickly became a life raft, and I clung to the idea. "This will work," I told my husband again and again. "This is the thing that will let all of us be happy here."

We made an offer, and it was accepted. I smiled as we signed the paperwork, but my husband was far less pleased. "I still don't know if this is a good idea," he told me that morning, his face dark with worry. But still, he signed, knowing he didn't have a better plan. "I'm trusting your judgment," he said as we made plans to move in. "I don't feel confident about any of this. But you're so sure, and I'm going to trust you."

No pressure, I told myself. "It's going to work," I responded. And by some combination of foresight and fortune, it did.

My husband loves the house and the neighbourhood and will now say without hesitation that it was the right decision for our family. I no longer feel homesick all the time. The kids are thriving, and my mom loves the basement suite. My career picked back up as my depression faded away, and my husband found a new job that all but eliminated his daily commute. The darkness that had weighed on us both lifted, revealing the kind of life we'd planned when we first set out together so many years ago.

I don't remember much about our time in the first house. For whatever reason, my brain has decided to protect me from reliving that chapter. Sometimes I forget we were ever there. When I think about where we lived before this house, I picture our place in Toronto, not the stressful in-between.

I never would have chosen the suburbs, but I'm grateful for them now. I don't feel the same ache in my heart when I leave the city on the train, because I'm not so desperately out of place in my new life. The city is still my home, but so is my house on the court in a place that's not too far away. I can live—happily even—in both worlds.

Plus, when we retire one day, our nest empty, the house larger than we want or need? There might be a condo in the city that calls us back. Until then, I can wait.

YOU'RE NOT SUPERWOMAN
AND THAT'S OKAY

A never-ending stream of information plays inside my head, like the news ticker on a weather station. It updates constantly, sometimes with new information and sometimes repeating itself, daring me to take it all in without forgetting. It lists household tasks and work deadlines, social obligations and the particulars of my kids' entire lives. It reminds me to make dinner, sign field trip forms, replace worn-out shoes, and keep up with the pediatrician's recommended vaccination schedule. I hurry to make notes and add dates to calendars so I don't forget, but the volume of information is relentless. Inevitably, I miss something or otherwise screw up. I whisper apologies to everyone around me.

When you look at any single item on this list, it seems relatively easy to cross off. We're not talking about complicated stuff—every task is mundane, and yet they keep piling up in order to take over my life.

Plan meals, make the grocery list, then figure out when you have time to go to the store. Don't forget to buy coffee while you're there. Remember that work deadline—it's an important one. Get the kids' bags ready for swim lessons and send an e-transfer to the piano teacher. Clean out the fridge and the microwave, or at least one of them, because they're gross. Vacuum out the car, same reason. Get gas while you're out. Buy a gift for that birthday party and have the kids make a card. Book haircuts for your increasingly dishevelled offspring. Book a haircut for yourself and then cancel because it conflicts with something the kids have. Put wine in the fridge so you can offer it to guests later. Switch the laundry before it gets musty and has to be washed a second time. Or a third. Take chicken breasts out of the freezer soon or there'll be nothing for dinner. Find a photo of the family for that school project. Make lunches for tomorrow. Replace the soap in the washroom. Water the plants.

On and on it goes, forever, and then one day you're dead.

I am the person in our family who knows where everything is, except for my own phone and sunglasses. I am the keeper of schedules, birthdays, school events, and big feelings. I am the problem solver. I am our chief medical officer and emergency task force. I make and execute plans and deal with unexpected challenges as they arise.

One day last year, my daughter came home and announced that one of her classmates had lice. "Did they check you?" I asked quickly, a shudder running down my spine at the idea of live bugs on her head.

She nodded. "I don't have it—they checked everyone."

They had, and she was fine—until the following week, when she came home and sat at the kitchen table, a concerned look on her face. "Mama," she started slowly. "My head itches."

I froze in place. "Nooooooo. Really?"

She nodded. "Can you check my hair?"

I did, quickly finding what looked like eggs. "Oh," I said, trying and failing to stay cool. "You totally have lice."

I thought about what I had planned for the rest of the day—cooking dinner, running a couple errands once the kids were in bed, working on an article that was due soon. That was all about to be pushed back in favour of combing out my child's conditioner-soaked hair with a fine-tooth nit pick. I'd do a lot of that over the next week, also taking her for professional nit removal and then combing out her hair at home again and again as the lice travelled enthusiastically around the heads of her classmates, hitting several of them a second time.

"My teacher wore her hair in a ponytail for the first time today," my daughter remarked drily.

"Are you bothered by any of this?" I asked her, thinking of how embarrassed I would have been at her age.

She shrugged. "Nah, not really. Maybe if I was the only one, but like, everyone has it now."

I was proud of how unflappable she was, and deeply relieved that no one else in our house was affected.

This has happened to us with pink eye (everyone got it), gastroenteritis (we all went down), and strep throat (an infection that's worse for adults than kids, which I learned the hard way). At one point, the kids and I all had ear infections, which was baffling because those aren't even contagious. "It probably started from a shared cold," the doctor said, shrugging and writing us a series of prescriptions. Through it all, the ticker in my head kept ticking, reminding me of everything that had to get done for our house to operate. There were still dinners to make and deadlines to hit. Life doesn't stop—it just gets more complicated.

I've discovered that even when you're too sick to do it all, you're still doing it all: calling the school to say the kids will be home sick, making doctor's appointments, cancelling piano lessons for the week, or popping out to fill a prescription. Occasionally delegating these things to your husband, who is willing to do anything you ask but needs to be asked. He'll notice a sink full of dirty dishes and clean them without a word, but a trip to the grocery store requires direction akin to a military mission. Plan A, Plan B, and, if possible, notes on where to find unfamiliar items in the store.

"I don't have time to be sick," I always moan. This is because for me, there are no true days off—tasks just pile up until they're addressed or abandoned.

Even when everyone is healthy and things are going well, the list marches on. I often wonder how single moms do it all. I have a partner who is present, engaged, and devoted to our family, and I'm still exhausted most of the time. The mental load is enormous. My husband would never think to check if the kids' underwear still fits or if they need new socks. I don't know if he'd ever think to wash stuffed animals or purge old toys and clothes as they grow out of them. It's likely there'd be no teacher gifts, Christmas cards, or holiday photos. He'd provide the necessities of life, but ask him what the kids' shoe sizes are or what Santa usually puts in their stockings and he'd be lost.

He's far from lazy and often putters around with a broom in his hands, tidying up and throwing in laundry as he moves through the house. He gets up with the kids in the morning, handles bedtime like a champion, and takes them to swimming lessons. He is what most people would consider a good dad and a good husband—I certainly think this—and even so, we all rely on my brain to keep our household moving. I'm the executive with the plan and my husband is a capable administrator who waits for direction. He understands the kids need to eat; I'm the one who knows both their preferences and what's in the fridge. He might pack sunscreen for a day out; I'm the one who knows which brand of sunscreen gives our son a rash, which one doesn't, and which we haven't tried. He does things very well, but usually only after I've laid out what needs to be done.

It's been suggested to me that if managing my household leaves me so exhausted, I should lower my standards. I should stop sending Christmas cards if it's so much work, skip teacher gifts, quit volunteering at the school, or "let the house be a mess." The latter is only said by those who don't know me well, because the house is a mess most of the time. So is my car. If I get seventy percent of my list done, the rest is readily ignored. This means the garbage in my car, the laundry pile beside my bed, and the pile of paperwork in my office all sit there, taunting me everywhere I go.

But these other things, the nice-to-haves, are important to me. I don't want the bare minimum from life, I want to live the hell out of it. I love our holiday traditions, like the visit to Santa and the photo cards. I want to recognize the teachers who devote so much of their time and energy to my children. I care about finding the right sunscreen for my sensitive-skinned child. Volunteering in the school brings me joy. I want to do it all. I cannot turn off this element of my personality, nor do I want to. I have never done anything halfway, except for cleaning my house. That, I always do halfway.

There are items I've chopped off the list and expectations I've skirted, but I'm selective about what those things are. My children don't participate in a ton of extracurriculars because it requires more money and time than I'm willing to spend. We pick and choose how to spend our time, placing value on what matters to us, not to others. Despite this, there is always somewhere to be and plenty to do.

Some families love hockey or happily run between three soccer games a week, but that's not for us. Similarly, some families couldn't care less about the things that matter to mine. It doesn't matter how you spend your time as a family, as long as you're doing what you want instead of what others expect of you. I prioritize a sit-down dinner every night. Other parents prioritize something else. Neither approach is better, they're just different ways of dividing time and creating happiness. I prefer to be home after school and on weekends, or out hiking with my family. As overextended as I sometimes am, I'm guarded with my time and energy.

Moms are always working, inside the house or out, their brains always in high gear. We do as much parenting as previous generations and then some, with the rise of extracurriculars and parent councils and Pinterest, and it's now the norm for moms to work full-time jobs outside the home. We don't parent less if we work more—we just sleep fewer hours and get less downtime. Burnout isn't extraordinary, it's incredibly common and very real. The standards set for modern motherhood are absolutely impossible and set us up to fail. There's a pervasive mentality that we have to do it all, be it all, keep a thousand balls in the air at one time, and it's killing us.

We're told to make time for ourselves and prioritize self-care. But how? Where do we find the time, the money, the energy? Self-care was a phrase that once held meaning in political spaces as a form of self-preservation and resistance. Popularized by Audre Lorde, the term spoke directly to marginalized communities, but in recent years it's been stolen by brands to sell things like face masks, bath bombs, and spa days. Manicures are suddenly self-care. Wine is always lauded as self-care. I enjoy many of those things, but I know this isn't what Lorde meant. Bath bombs don't buy me more time in my day, relieve my invisible workload, or check items off my to-do list. Treating ourselves well shouldn't have to mean spending money. Participating in capitalism isn't self-care, no matter what we're told over and over again. It's okay to enjoy these things, but let's not lie to ourselves about what they do for us. A pedicure does not make up for six months of disrupted sleep with a new baby or a lifetime of being overworked and underpaid. Ask a single mom what would make her life better. I doubt the answer is something you can order online.

A weekend away with your partner or friends is a wonderful treat, but it doesn't solve our problems. It's an escape rather than a solution. It's also a lot of extra work to plan and execute a trip, sinking you further into the stress that makes you want to take a break in the first place.

I flew to Chicago for a bachelorette party in 2018, when my kids were six and eight years old. And by "party" I mean a multi-day trip to another country, because that was what the bride wanted. It was an amazing four days of touring the city, dining out, dancing, and visiting comedy clubs. I got dressed up (not really dressed up, more so I didn't wear plain black leggings every day) and wasn't responsible for anyone but myself and, occasionally, the bride (as the maid of honour, I felt responsible for both her well-being and enjoyment of the trip). It was lovely. Even the plane ride itself felt like a vacation. I read a book for two uninterrupted hours. At this point in my life, I welcome a long flight alone; it is truly not the inconvenience it used to be.

But for that trip to happen, I had to make sure my husband blocked off his schedule so he could parent solo for four days. Then I made arrangements for my mother to pick up the kids after school and watch them for a few hours while my husband was still at work. I made sure they had enough groceries and stocked the freezer with convenience foods like lasagna and frozen pizza. I told both teachers I'd be away, so if an emergency occurred, they'd reach out to my husband instead of me. I worked double my usual number of freelance hours the week before so I could justify taking a few days off, snuck in extra cuddles with the kids, and, finally, packed my bags. Oh, and I planned the bachelorette party itself, booking accommodations for the group, collaborating on planned activities, and buying penis-themed decorations. If ever I didn't want customs going through my suitcase, it was that weekend. My bag was, quite literally, full of dicks.

Planning any sort of getaway is a big deal when you have kids, but in the end, it was all worth it. I came home remembering what it was like to feel young and (almost) carefree, even if my kids were in the back of my mind the entire time. I was also incredibly happy to get home to a life dominated by sweatpants and falling asleep in a single bed beside one of my children, snuggled up after bedtime songs and stories, my hair a mess and no champagne to be found. I do not belong in a carefree world anymore, nor do I want to. I'm not chasing another life. I just need my own life to slow down sometimes.

The ticker in my head will probably always keep going, but I'm trying to tame it. In a way, the most effective form of self-care I've discovered is saying the word *no*. Not because I'm giving up on what matters to me, but because I'm prioritizing it. No, you can't have more of my time and energy than I'm reasonably able to give. No, I won't go to every event or send my kids to every birthday party, because sometimes I want to stay in my pyjamas and hang out with my family until two in the afternoon doing nothing. They won't be in four activities each and have play dates every weekend. I'll volunteer for some things but not everything. I'll skip the bake sale when I'm busy at work instead of baking two dozen cookies at midnight, even when I want to say yes. And sure, sometimes I'll do the self-care things that aren't really self-care—the bath bombs, the pedicures, the face masks—because they don't solve my problems, but they do relax me, however briefly. My life is just as hectic with manicured nails, but it's a pleasant interlude at least.

I've also found power in saying yes. Yes to my village—I accept the help you're offering because I cannot and should not do it all. I'm grateful for you, and I'm there for you in return. Yes to my husband when he offers to do something in my place, even though I know he won't do it the way I want him to, and that makes me squirm like the control freak I fully am. Yes to admitting I'm having a long week and need to talk about it. Yes to acknowledging that we aren't meant to do this alone. And yes, yes, yes, I'll do that thing that's purely for fun because it's okay to do things for myself. We all need to have fun. Life is meant to be enjoyed, and I'm ready to enjoy it. What better example can I set for my kids than that?

PLACES I HAVE FAILED

One crisp, sunny fall day when my children were maybe four and five years old, my husband and I decided to take them to one of our favourite hiking spots in Ontario's greenbelt: a lush, beautiful, mosquito-filled haven. We often went there to let them run around the trail, collect walking sticks, and look for bears (of course, there are no bears in the area). They liked to refer to themselves not as hikers but as "adventurers," roaming the forest in search of something wild and amazing. So, after encouraging everyone to use the washroom and packing a bag full of water bottles and granola bars, I'd toss out the usual threats related to getting along in the car, and off we'd go.

Driving north along Brant Street in Burlington, we stopped at a red light next to a Catholic school on the corner. We'd passed this spot a million times, but for some reason my son was just noticing it for the first time. "Mama," he began quizzically. "Why is that man up there on that T?"

I looked up to where he was pointing, confused, and then I saw it: a huge, wooden cross with a depiction of Jesus Christ splayed across it, adorning the church next to the school. I didn't know whether to laugh or cry that my then-five-year-old child didn't know who Jesus was.

We are not religious, but I was raised in a churchgoing family, and my maternal grandfather was a highly respected United Church of Canada minister. My grandpa and I were very close—in many ways, he was more like a father than a grandparent to me—and my parents brought us to church services every Sunday during my childhood. I was told that God was real, and I believed this to be true for some time. I said my prayers occasionally before bed and hoped I wouldn't end up in hell for fighting with my siblings. I joined the church choir, attended Sunday school, and had a confirmation ceremony around age ten. Then, as I grew up, my views on religion slowly evolved from "My mom says God is real, so he must be," to "I have some serious questions about all of this," to "Yeah, I'm definitely an atheist."

While my mother was dismayed by this news and still believes it to be some form of rebellion rather than grounded in genuine consideration, my grandparents were quite supportive when I shared my views. "I'm agnostic myself," my grandmother said warmly as her minister husband shrugged. My grandpa believed in the church, but he was a progressive, critical thinker who loved a good academic discussion. We went on to have many conversations about the idea of God and the Trinity, and what they meant to him. "It's not all literal, of course," he'd say of the Bible. "They are stories meant to guide us. What lessons can we take from them?"

My husband didn't grow up with any significant connection to a church, which was probably one of the factors that led to him majoring in religious studies in university (he also majored in peace studies, which is a real thing despite the confused response of ninety percent of people who ask what his degree is in). He took classes on various world religions and studied each doctrine as someone with an interest in the history and impact of organized religion, but post-graduation, we both learned that many people assumed religious studies was a euphemism for theology. "No, he's not going to be a minister," I've patiently told dozens of people. "He's actually an atheist."

"Then why study religion?" People asked this with genuine interest or amusement.

"Well," I'd reply, "religion is a major part of how the world works. It influences law and politics and has led to wars, and often guides how people in society interact with one another." Usually, they'd nod and move on, satisfied and/ or bored—yet another reason why religion doesn't make a good subject for conversation at parties.

When we got married, my grandpa conducted a secular ceremony for us without hesitation. "No G-word, no J-word" were our instructions, and he smirkingly agreed, though my sister insisted on reading a popular passage from 1 Corinthians as an homage to the movie *Wedding Crashers*. We chose not to baptize our children when they were born—a decision that many people thought would upset my grandfather. Instead, he showed unwavering support. "You don't believe in God," he said simply. "Why would you baptize them when it's meaningless to you, and you're not going to raise them as members of the Church?"

"It's a holy ceremony, not a party," he continued. "I see people do it all the time and then never once bring their kids to a church service. In those cases, it often makes more sense not to do it. I think you've made the right choice for your family."

He sometimes called me his Godless granddaughter, but always with affection, and I believe we talked about religion with more seriousness and frequency than any other members of the family. In a way, having an atheist grandchild gave him a greater opportunity for deep discussions of his views. He loved the mystery of God and the philosophical elements of Christianity, as well as the strong community-building activities and the church's connection to music. He sat on interfaith councils and spent decades fighting for civil rights, including gay marriage and rights for openly gay ministers. He made sure to use the correct pronouns with his non-binary colleague. When, after much soul-searching, a fellow United Church minister came out as atheist, my grandfather was contemplative. "It raises some big questions about what a minister is, and she must have done a lot of reflection to come to this place," he told me thoughtfully, interested in the story but not passing judgment.

My husband and I had vowed to teach our kids about a wide range of religions so that one day they could make their own informed decisions about their beliefs. Maybe they'd be atheists like us, or they'd find a religion that felt right to them. We hoped that exposing them to a variety of beliefs would be the most balanced and inclusive approach—and crossed our fingers that neither of them would end up in a cult.

Driving past the church that day, I realized we'd failed. *Why is that man up there on that T?* Not only did my son have no idea what a crucifix was, but he didn't know who Jesus was—one of the most recognizable figures in the world. And it wasn't like he'd seen a cartoon image of Christ out of context; he was attached to the front of the church on a massive cross.

We hadn't done what we'd set out to do, and I felt genuinely bad about it.

We weren't going to start taking our kids to church. We had, however, agreed to expose them to all sorts of different religions and give them a sense that each one had merit and value. Then life got busy, and we hadn't put much effort into teaching them anything about, well, anything religious. They knew some of their friends' moms wore hijabs for religious reasons, that a teacher celebrated Hanukkah because she was Jewish, and they'd been to exactly one Diwali party. But if you'd asked them to explain one thing about any of the religions associated with these events, including the Christianity their grandparents took part in? Crickets.

We'd been better at raising the kids to be inclusive than informed, I realized. Our kids understood that some people were religious, and others were not, and so we started by teaching them that every religion was special to the people who were active in it, and therefore should be spoken about with respect. "I don't believe in God, but Grammie does," I told them over dinner one day. "Papa Donnie does too, and I respect their beliefs. There's nothing wrong with believing in God."

A good start, I figured, until my daughter asked me to clarify. "What is God? Like, what are God and Jesus?"

I took a deep breath, not wanting to screw up. "Christians—"

"What are Christians?" my son interjected. This was getting worse.

"Christians are people who practise Christianity. Like the Catholic Church and a lot of Protestant Churches. The United Church is a Christian organization."

"Anyway," I went on. "Christians believe that God is an almighty spirit that sees and knows everything about the world, even though people can't see him. They believe God created the world and loves them, which is why they pray. Sometimes they pray because they're grateful, or because they're sad or frustrated and feel like they need answers. So you can't see God, but some people believe in him and feel him and take comfort in that, and that's why they attend church. So they can read the Bible, which is about God, and talk about it, and give thanks."

This spilled out awkwardly but in earnest, and my children listened attentively. "And who is Jesus?"

"God's son, but he wasn't a spirit. He was a real man but then he was crucified—like, killed on a cross, which is why you see him like that at the church—and people believe he came back to life, but then went back to be with God. So he's very special in Christianity."

My kids sat quietly, looking thoughtful. I waited expectantly, hoping I'd explained things well enough and with the respect I intended. "Well," my daughter began slowly. "I doubt many people actually believe *that*."

"Oh," I quickly replied, flustered. "They do though. A lot of people believe that and it's very important to them. Like, millions of people. It's an extremely common belief."

"Huh," she said, unmoved.

The kids wandered off, no longer interested, leaving me feeling zero percent better about my ability to educate them on religion. My husband and I would laugh about this later, amused by our daughter's dismissal of God as something very few people would believe in (she was in for a surprise) and by our son's description of Jesus as a man on a T.

"They're young," I consoled myself. "We still have time to make up for this."

And we did. But as the years went on, I realized our inclusive approach to child-rearing was lacking in several other departments. Our kids were familiar with the concept of marriage and knew that while they had heterosexual parents, some couples were comprised of two men or two women. The first time my son noticed a rainbow flag on the street, he asked what it was for. "It's a gay pride flag," I replied. "It shows that you believe people should be able to love who they love, regardless of gender."

Later, one of my kids would reference this conversation, saying, "I can marry anyone I want because of the rainbow flag!" Which, while simplistic, isn't off the mark.

I explained words like *transgender* and *nonbinary* in an effort to normalize them. I helped them understand that some people are born in the wrong body and have to take steps to be recognized for their true gender, and that some people don't feel like they're either male or female.

I felt like I was doing a decent job raising them to be good people who would treat others kindly regardless of colour, religion, or sexuality. I led with kindness and compassion and hoped that this example would be a good foundation to tackling bigger questions later in life. As a family, we still speak openly about how people are all different and that's okay, because our differences often make the world a better and more interesting place.

Growing up, my grandparents had a rainbow triangle magnet on their fridge and plenty of gay friends, and we were always taught that all people are equal. They hired handymen who had been in jail because "everyone makes mistakes, and we don't know how they ended up there." They were compassionate to homeless people, always offering them food and a few kind words, and took us to volunteer at a local shelter. My mom in particular believed in a "colour-blind" approach to race and would never have stood for anything racist or homophobic to be said in our house. This was absolutely a better approach than many of the alternatives that I saw in the homes of my friends and even extended family members. But however well-intentioned, in hindsight I can see how this approach is problematic.

When we moved to a small town when I was eleven, I first witnessed racism, homophobia, and other acts of hate targeting Indigenous and Black people. It was horrifying, and I was shocked. Having grown up in a bubble where equality was touted as the norm, I had always looked at racism and homophobia as past-tense things—as in, people used to be racist and homophobic, but now people know better, and everyone lives together in harmony.

Yes, I was that fucking naive. It's called white privilege, and I have it in spades.

Living in that rural community, I heard the N-word for the first time—and then many more times—and was quickly overwhelmed by the realization that racism very much remained a current issue. I arrived home from school one day upset that another student had been saying terrible, racist things during a casual conversation, and my neighbour asked what was wrong. When I tearfully recounted what had been said and how I'd been mocked for trying to stop it, the neighbour quickly erupted into her own racist tirade. Instead of the horror I'd expected her to react with, I was met with more hate.

There was a reason many of the kids in that town were racist—it started at home, so of course I wasn't about to find support from their parents. I walked into my house and never spoke to that neighbour again. The next few years were eye-opening, to say the least.

This is where inclusivity isn't nearly enough and colour-blindness fails. My well-meaning family spoke about treating all people with love, but they'd neglected to tell me that not all families felt the same way. When we did talk about racism, it was addressed as something rare, unacceptable, and universally abhorred. I had no idea hate was so rampant solely because it was never aimed at me, and as a result I was shocked when I first saw hate aimed at other people. It's taken years for me to fill in the gaps in my understanding, and I understand now this learning is a lifelong process.

In being raised to believe that all people are equal, and ethnicity doesn't matter, I was taught to look past everyday racism. I didn't see skin colour have a direct effect on how a person experiences the world, because I'd been taught that skin colour didn't matter. I wasn't aware of the biases that exist within all of us, or how those translate into different thoughts and actions. I had no idea what a microaggression was or how many subtle acts of racism were happening all around me. Some of my closest friends in childhood were Black or brown, and I genuinely had no idea they were treated any differently by society than I was until we were basically adults.

I didn't understand racism as an ongoing problem, so I hadn't thought about how to stand up to it. This was true with homophobia and other hateful biases too. I eventually educated myself and grew to be vocal against these injustices, trying hard to identify my own weaknesses and learn from them. I'm still learning, and always will be, and I'm determined that my own children won't be as sheltered as I was.

But even so, there are times I've failed. My kids might have loved "the rainbow flag" and been able to define *trans* and *nonbinary*, but I hadn't shared the harms that are inflicted on those communities.

A few of my daughter's feminist reference books mention women of colour persevering against racism, so I asked her if she knew what racism meant. "Not really," she replied. She understood that they'd gone through something hard but hadn't made the connection between hardship and ethnicity.

I asked my son if he knew what racism or homophobia meant. "Nope," he quickly replied. Oof. I have so much work to do.

Shortly after this, in June 2020, a Black Lives Matter march took place in our neighbourhood. I'd been making more of an effort to talk to the kids about racism and systemic injustice. I wanted them to understand how important the march was and how change couldn't happen without people like them making it happen. That said, this was also the early stage of a global pandemic, and I had three high-risk individuals living in my house, including myself and my son. Joining the group was out of the question, I decided, though I wanted to be there. Instead, we watched the march go by from a distance, clapping in support, and I explained the different messages as they were shouted out. "Black Lives Matter!" we heard again and again, and then, "No justice, no peace!"

I tried to walk the line between age appropriate and honest, emphasizing how necessary it is to stand up against hate. "We are white, so we don't experience racism," I explained. "But it's really, really important that we tell other people that racism is not okay. You cannot just let it happen because it doesn't affect you. We have privilege because we're white, and you have to use that privilege for good."

My son was thoughtful, then referenced one of his non-white friends. "If someone ever said something mean to Steven, I'd tell them that's wrong."

"That's a good start," I told him. "But there's a lot more we can do."

When I first had my babies, I held them in my arms with huge hopes and dreams for their futures. Like every mom, I wanted to keep them safe and warm, protect them from sadness or harm. I wanted them to grow, thrive, and have amazing lives. Holding them like that, I didn't stop to think about all the other moms with the same hopes and dreams who knew how much harder the world would be on their kids. Now I think about those moms all the time.

The gaps in my understanding didn't come from a lack of care—good people have plenty of faults. I'm trying to do better. My kids will know more about racism and homophobia than I did as a child, because they can't fight against something they don't understand. I may never get it perfectly right, but the world is on fire and my job is to teach them that it's not okay to be complacent or look away. I will teach my kids that being "not racist" isn't the same as being anti-racist. This is a promise I'm making to them and to myself, because it's the bare minimum I can do.

WHY MOMMY DRINKS

It's a beautiful evening in early June, one of the first truly lovely nights of the year. The spring air is still pleasantly warm long after the dinner hour, the sky valiantly resisting the urge to go dark. I've spent the last several hours curled up in an outdoor chair, my legs tucked under me, surrounded by friends in similar positions. Our boisterous conversation has broken down into smaller, more intimate discussions that blend together and form a pleasant, relaxing hum. Our voices fill the yard and drift into neighbouring spaces, heads leaning in closer to one another as confidences are quietly shared, bursts of laughter punctuating the gentle buzz. Everyone lingers well past the time they'd planned on being home in bed, not only for the wondrous quality of night sky and fresh air after a long winter, but because we're among friends, a joy in and of itself.

Eventually someone makes a move to leave and the rest of us follow, collecting sweaters and plastic wineglasses as we go. On the walk home, I am slightly buzzed, a half-empty bottle of rosé sticking out of my purse. My friends all carry similar bottles—our host didn't need a dozen partially consumed bottles of wine, she insisted, telling us to take them with us. A few people hold empty vessels they'll drop into blue bins as they arrive home. One friend, the only teetotaller in the group, offers a ride, though most of us choose to wander home on foot, finishing conversations and giggling in the dark.

Walking into my kitchen a little while later, I stick the remaining wine in the fridge and sigh at how much is left, knowing it'll grow stale and I'll end up pouring it down the sink. If it were red or even white, my husband might finish the bottle for me, but he has little interest in the sweetness of rosé. Maybe I'll have another glass tomorrow, I think, even as I know I won't.

I don't know many people who'd admit to wanting to drink more, and it's certainly not a goal I have—but I sometimes find myself wondering how my drinking pattern compares to other that of other moms. I think about this for two reasons: first, I come from a family where alcoholism is not not an issue, and second, because popular culture seems to demand that as a mom, I should be pounding back wine on a nightly basis.

But I don't.

I am not a hashtag wine mom, though I am a mom who sometimes drinks wine. I've come to learn that these are two very different things. Consuming alcohol, for me, is a pleasurable but infrequent event. Every once in a while, I have a drink with my husband, which takes me about an hour to finish because I'm a slow sipper and an active talker. The normal number of alcoholic beverages I have in a given week is zero, but if I go out with friends, that number may shoot up to a whopping two or three. I get tipsy at weddings, our annual block party, and the odd holiday gathering, but have only been truly drunk a handful of times.

I suppose this makes me a social drinker. I like a bit of cold, dry white wine on a patio, or a gin and soda at a party, but I can just as easily go without it. I've never gone out of my way to get a drink, but I will often say yes when one is offered to me. I almost never drink alone. At one point—when I'd been pregnant, then nursing, then pregnant again, then nursing forever because my second child didn't want to wean—I realized I hadn't had a drop of alcohol in almost four years. I can't say I missed it.

I am only marginally less sober now. This is apparently a great accomplishment, as the world is hell-bent on telling me to rely on wine to get through daily life with my children. Wine is sold to me as a crutch for every struggle, however large or small, presented as the fuel necessary to exist as a woman and parent in a time when both roles are unfairly scrutinized. Alcohol is supposed to give me something to look forward to while helping me forget the less-than-ideal times. It's supposed to be fun—and yet, the more I'm told I should want or need to drink, the less I do.

I have no moral opposition to drinking alcohol, but I have long felt a persistent discomfort with wine-mom culture. I don't like what it implies about motherhood—that it's something to be survived—or the way it masks or deflects our problems. There's nothing wrong with enjoying a glass or even a bottle of wine as an escape, barring addiction or dependency, but there's something unsettling about the way drinking is used to distract us from what makes us want to escape in the first place.

Women are constantly told to be more and do more, which creates a never-ending list of tasks to be executed wholly and without complaint. We are always on the clock. We are to work hard, nurture everyone around us, manage a household, care for our aging parents, support our husbands, and ignore the overwhelming weight of the patriarchy while looking good and making it all appear easy. We are handed a mountain of responsibility, and when we question our ability to scale it independently, we're offered a glass of red instead of a practical solution. Wine is not the problem, we're told, it's the cure. Wine is self-care. It's the secret to making it through this life, so go ahead and fill your glass until your troubles fade. Motherhood isn't easy, so drink up.

We could ask mothers to speak up instead, of course, but it's so much easier to offer them a drink. "I need a glass of wine" has replaced important phrases in our vocabulary and stopped conversations before they begin. We've lost "I need help," "I need to talk," and "I'm really struggling right now"; instead, we fill a glass. Mom culture tells us this is normal, but it's not. I cringe when I think of all the times a friend has ordered a drink with a wry comment about their day and I've nodded encouragingly over a generous pour, letting the real questions remain unasked. "There you go," I've said. "You've earned it."

Earned what, exactly? When we speak in code and build walls around what we really mean to say, we prevent people from connecting the way they need to. We watch women being eaten alive by a culture that demands too much from them and places little value on their health or joy. We see them drowning but instead of offering a life jacket, we pour them another drink; we keep filling the bucket they're drowning in.

I want to hear more of the truth, with or without a wine-glass on the table. Tell me you had a hard day because you're overwhelmed at work, worried about a family member, or argued with your partner. Tell me you yelled at your kids and feel like a bad mom. Let me know that one of your kids is struggling, or you're struggling, or your marriage is struggling. Explain how parenting has been harder than usual and you feel like a failure. You don't need to lay yourself bare but say *something*. Speak the words that catch in your throat instead of washing them down as if they don't exist.

I sometimes think of a woman I knew who survived abuse, grew up to have children, and became an alcoholic. Her drinking was not cute or fun; it was sad and scary and created a world of pain for her children, who fell into the same cycle of abuse. This was not a wine mom. This was a mother and an alcoholic. But what's the difference? Like other moms, she was told to drink up and push on through. She did what we're all told to do—but then she crossed the line that transformed her habit from charming to tragic. Wine-mom jokes aren't endearing if made about people with actual substance abuse issues. So why are they cute when made about others? I don't want any part in it.

I'm scared that as wine-mom culture becomes more pervasive, honest conversations between acquaintances will come to feel strange—if they happen at all. I worry that actual drinking problems will be harder to recognize because we've conditioned ourselves to drink in the bad times as well as the good. We are normalizing pain and accepting a solution that doesn't actually solve anything. We're told how to live and parent (grit your teeth and drink later) and what our coping mechanisms should be (more wine). We conflate motherhood and addiction while creating a social club that excludes sober women. We're telling all mothers to drink, whether it's problematic for them or not.

When I hear kids referred to as the reason Mommy drinks, even jokingly, I want to grab the person and say, "No—your kids are not the reason you drink. Don't tell yourself that. Don't let that be where you lay blame for your stress or unhappiness. This is about other things." The completely unrealistic expectations placed on women and mothers may be why you drink. Societies that control and punish women might be the reason you drink. Or maybe, like me, you just have kids and enjoy a drink sometimes, and those two truths are not directly connected. These are luxuries we afford men, so why not claim them for ourselves?

Another warm evening, another backyard filled with friends, conversation, and drink glasses that are filled and emptied and filled again. I'm here because I enjoy this—not just the wine, but the companionship these nights offer. I am happy and relaxed, enjoying the taste of wine and the steady emergence of stars overhead.

My family is not something I have to suffer or bear, and motherhood is not something I numb myself to survive. I never drink because I need to, or because my children have driven me to numb myself. To suggest otherwise is an insult to me and to them. I may sometimes fill my cup, but not as a means of coping. When things get hard, there are better ways for me to take care of myself. Tonight, I'm just having fun.

MY JOB IS NOT A HOBBY

I wasn't a little girl who dreamed of her wedding day, though modern rom-coms would have us believe this is something all little girls do. I liked the idea of romance as much as the next late-nineties tween who watched *My Girl* and sobbed into her pillow, but I never fantasized about the white dress or settling down. Instead, I dreamed of the career I'd have when I was older—I'd be a writer or a lawyer, or maybe both, if I was lucky—I pictured myself smartly dressed and capable in court or wrapped in a cardigan at a large wooden desk, a stained-glass lamp beside me as I wrote late into the night. I loved the idea of work: the challenges and ideas and opportunities to create things. There was an allure to the grown-up life that drew me in, but it wasn't about who I'd end up with. It was who I could be.

I wanted a spacious home office that doubled as a library. Watching *Beauty and the Beast* as a child, I remember thinking how messed up it was that Belle fell in love with her kidnapper, but also, damn, that library. I also knew I wanted to be a mom one day. I took for granted that motherhood was inevitable, and instead I spent time considering things like travel and a career. When you're a child, so many decisions are made for you. I wanted to see the world and make decisions for myself.

There are days when I'm surprised how close I've come to making my early goals happen. I'm not a lawyer, but I studied law for four years as an undergrad before deciding an LLB wasn't for me. I am a writer—albeit not one with a private library or a stack of bestselling books to my name—and I'm satisfied by this career path. I'm not completely living my dreams, but I'm happy and still relatively young, with time to do more. I could end up with a beautiful home library one day (a more reasonable update on Belle's haunted mansion version), and if I don't, that's okay. I've done well for myself. But I sometimes wonder how much further along I'd be without the struggles that come with being a working mom.

After my first child was born, I had to figure out how work fit into my new life as a parent. I'd freelanced as a writer for several years and appreciated the flexibility it afforded, so I continued to take on small jobs to keep a seat at the table and contribute toward paying our bills. At the time, we lived in a modest apartment that was mostly underground, so our expenses weren't outrageous. My husband had been recently promoted, and his job now provided financial security for our little family. This meant that money I made helped, but it wasn't essential for us to get by. As someone who grew up with a single mom who struggled financially, getting by made me feel rich.

I remember sitting at a small glass table in our apartment, my newborn curled up on a nursing pillow and a laptop set up in front of me. She breastfed while I quietly typed, answering emails and writing copy for carpet manufacturers and financial websites. Editorial assignments were few and far between, but copywriting provided me with a steady stream of gigs. I didn't work a lot, but I did work, and when my second child was born a year later, I kept at it. I had no mat leave, since I was self-employed, so instead I worked a little bit here and there, often with a baby attached to my body or sleeping nearby.

It wasn't easy, but it felt good to use the work part of my brain, no matter how tired I was. I liked cashing cheques that came in my name, not my husband's. I craved a sliver of financial independence, however small. Work didn't feel like a chore—it was a privilege, something to keep me anchored to who I'd always been while I was discovering myself as a mother. No part of me wanted to give this up.

When friends felt differently about their jobs, complaining about the monotony, the workload, or wanting to retire early to escape the grind, I couldn't relate. I loved working and wanted to do more of it, not less.

I continued freelancing on a part-time basis until my youngest started junior kindergarten when he was just three and a half. Then, with both kids in school and hours of free time suddenly laid out before me, I dove back into my career, setting regular work hours while taking on new clients. I wrote more web copy and advertisements, prepared blog posts for small business owners, and began pitching editorial content again. Soon I was landing pieces in magazines I'd read for years, thrilled to see my byline onscreen and in print. Every small win felt amazing and motivated me to do more. After years of worrying it would be unrealistic for me to get by as a freelancer, I found myself turning down jobs because I was consistently overbooked.

Life was good, but child care outside of school hours was a constant battle. During a trial run at an after-school program run by a local community centre, we walked in to find several five-year-olds crouched on top of a bookshelf they'd scaled while an oblivious staffer stared into space less than three metres away. One of the kids leapt to the ground, landing like a cat at our feet. Another afternoon, a group of young boys climbed to the top of a heavily vined pergola next to the playground, watching in amusement as their child care provider searched for them at ground level. There were flooded bathrooms, flipped snack tables, and more fistfights than a UFC event. Children were temporarily lost more than once, and one of the staffers couldn't tell two unrelated boys apart, no matter how long she cared for them.

The adults were never really in control, and every child in the program knew it. We ended up withdrawing the kids when we realized we were paying $900 a month for part-time care that provided more stress than support.

My husband's office hours didn't allow him to drop off or pick up the kids, and without after-school care this task now fell completely on me. It was the true double shift of parenthood in every sense of the word: kids and a full-time job, both demanding the best of me every day.

Summer rolled around, and we tried camp, which cost an arm and a leg but kept the kids busy for seven or eight hours a day. They'd come home wiped out but happy, regaling us with stories of art and sports and camp games played with their new friends. "We had so much fun today," my son would eagerly tell me, speaking a mile a minute about hiking and archery and water fights. My daughter breathlessly detailed how she caught a salamander and let a woodpecker eat seeds from her hand while the other kids fed chickadees and wrens.

"Didn't it peck you?" I asked, astonished.

"No, it was very gentle and came back a lot of times. My camp counsellor said she'd never seen a kid feed a woodpecker before!"

Camp was a win for everyone in our family: the kids loved it, and my husband and I were both able to work. I had a hard time swallowing the cost though. *Maybe I should just keep them home, spend more time with them, and work at night*, I'd think to myself, looking at my credit card bill. *I could work less for a few months, go down to part-time, then amp back up in the fall.*

The plan sounded nice in theory; I'd still work but have loads of time with my children, who were growing faster than I could wrap my head around. But while we'd save money by eliminating camp fees, we'd also lose some of my income. It would be difficult to scale back on work and then claw back those losses eight weeks later. And my work couldn't be done entirely at night, meaning that no matter what, I'd spend my days balancing parenting and deadlines and probably screwing up both, at least a bit.

Oh, and working late every single night would mean I'd be exhausted and less than fun to hang out with during the day. No, my kids were better off going to camp with their friends and enjoying quality time with us on weekends. We also had a whole week earmarked for a family vacation (unpaid time off for me, but well worth it for my sanity). My reasons for keeping them home all summer would be selfish—to save money and have them around more, even if I knew it would be more chaos than quality time—so I sucked it up and we paid for camp, feeling strangely guilty all the while.

Do men debate keeping their jobs over the summer? I asked myself, though I already knew the answer. Of course they didn't—they just worked, and child care fell into place, usually because the mother stayed home or arranged it. I was as entitled to employment as my husband and yet I was the only one feeling guilty about choosing to work. This was bullshit, and I hated that I couldn't shake the guilt I felt for doing something my husband had been doing since day one: providing for our family.

But still, the cost. I couldn't get over it.

"Four weeks of camp for two kids adds up to more than our monthly mortgage payment," I lamented to a friend. "And you still have to make lunch every night. We can make it work, but I can't get over how expensive it is to send kids to day camp. How do people on lower incomes afford this? Do they go into debt or just not work?"

I knew the answer to this one too. Every family is different, but in many cases day camp is financially out of reach. Which means that someone doesn't work—and that someone is almost always a mom.

My husband's job couldn't be more different than mine. He has benefits, a pension, and a union that defends his rights in the workplace. He takes five weeks of paid vacation every year and gets sick days. His job isn't easy, but it's secure and has a lot of perks. He's earned every promotion through hard work and dedication, but they were also made possible because he's a straight white man with a wife who stayed home with the kids so he could concentrate on his career. In terms of barriers in the career path, he's faced none.

I struggle with the knowledge that I'm a feminist and also a person who willingly put her career on the back-burner because it felt like the right thing to do. It was the best option for our family when I looked at us as a unit and not as individual people. I could argue that it made sense for me to stay home because my husband's job wasn't as flexible as mine or because I wanted to be home with my kids in those early years. Both of those statements are true, but I also got into freelance work partly because I enjoyed the flexibility and partly because, as a woman who wanted kids, I knew our lives would be easier if my career could flow around my children's needs. I knew I'd be expected to stay home—at least for a while—and that the world is designed in such a way that it would be noticed if I didn't. If my husband had stayed home as our children's primary caregiver, he would have been an anomaly—also, I don't know if we could have survived, since my earning potential was much less.

My husband and I both went to university, but as a man, he was promoted faster and paid more than I would have been had we taken the same career track. According to Statistics Canada, women in Canada make an average of eighty-seven cents for every dollar a man makes (and even less if the woman is Indigenous, disabled, or a person of colour). That's after years of improvement for women in the workplace, and it's not just an issue here: countries all over the world have similar wage disparities. Sure, it's illegal to pay women less than men for equivalent work, but the gender pay gap still exists. Jobs that are more likely to be held by women typically pay less, women are more likely to work part-time than men, and women are far more likely to take a break from work or stop working altogether to care for their children. This doesn't even touch on discrimination and other perennial challenges women face. Simply put, it's harder to build a career as a woman, especially if you're a mom. It doesn't matter how hard you work or how talented you are—you'll face more barriers than your male counterparts. If this sounds discouraging, that's because it is.

My financial contribution to our household has always felt like a complement to my husband's earnings. Even as the gap slowly closes between what he makes and what I bring in, we rely on the stability of his income when planning our lives. Every year, I still consider taking the summer off to save money and flex my work hours around our children's needs and school schedules.

"I have so much work to do this week and there's a PA day on Friday," I've said to my husband in frustration, wondering how I'll get it all done.

"I could take the day off," he offers. "But let me know now, because I'd have to talk to my boss tomorrow."

His offer is genuine, but I almost always say no. "Don't waste a vacation day," I tell him with a sigh, wanting to bank those for family trips or days I'm out of town. "I'll just rearrange my day. It's fine."

And then it *is* fine, especially as the kids grow older and more independent—but also it's not. Even with a job and a supportive husband, I'm the default parent. I'm a mom first, career woman second, forever. While there's no universe in which my kids aren't my first priority, I know that putting the kids first means different things when applied to men and women. My husband puts the kids first too, but he's allowed to do it in a way that doesn't affect his career.

I participate in this system myself. The practical part of

my brain won't allow my husband to use a vacation day when I can keep an eye on our kids and still get some work done. I can half-work, half-parent for a day and then put in five hours of writing and editing after dinner. This isn't the worst thing in the world, but it sometimes makes my career feel like a nice-to-have instead of something necessary or deserving of support. It's convenient for us as a family, but frustrating for me as a person with dreams and goals.

In 2019, my husband went to two conferences in another country. I attended one in Texas. Each time he was away, it was no big deal. We missed him, but life went on smoothly during his absence. When I left town, however, it was a different story—not at home, but everywhere else. At my conference, I was repeatedly asked who was looking after my kids, a question my husband has literally never faced. At home, friends and neighbours checked in on him, invited him for dinner, and regularly asked how he was managing with me gone—was he was counting down the minutes until my plane landed? He managed great—he always does. He may be a terrible cook, but he's completely capable of parenting our kids without me, and, honestly, the house is usually cleaner when I get back from a trip. But the difference in attitudes toward our work travel clearly demonstrated the ways we are both treated unfairly.

Is it bad that I like to work? Does it make me less of a woman, or a mom, that I enjoy having a career? I've struggled with this question and the guilt it brings, even as I tell myself the answer is no. What's bad is how women are made to feel like they have to choose, or that in order to have both, they have to sacrifice while their male partners succeed. My job is not a cute accessory. I make real money and pay real taxes. I am as worthy of value and respect as anyone else, but there's a decent chance I'll forever feel like support staff to my husband's CEO.

"Men don't like it when women make more money than they do," a talking head announces on a television show, and my husband snorts.

"I can't wait until you make more money than I do," he says earnestly. "I welcome you to make more money than me. My masculinity can handle it."

He means this, and I know he'd be more proud than insecure if I were suddenly the higher earner in our marriage. But what he also means is that he'll be happy if I make more money and also keep doing everything I do for our family. He's not saying he'd be happy if I worked longer hours at a job outside the house, stopped flexing my schedule around the kids, and delegated some of the invisible tasks of motherhood to him. I know he'd be supportive if I ever made this decision, but when he pictures me making more money, he's missing the full context of what that would entail. I'd need someone to support me the way I've supported him. I'd need a wife.

Even happy marriages with good men have these blind spots. I'm proof that understanding the problem isn't enough on its own to fix it. Progress often comes in inches, not miles, and we aren't there yet. But with every professional milestone I hit and every cheque I cash, I know I'm headed in the right direction. Even more so, I'm well aware of the example it sets for my children. Not just my daughter, who will have to break her own glass ceiling(s), but for my son, who should understand the value of having women in the workforce. We all deserve to chase our dreams, no matter what they are.

I love my work, and it doesn't make me any less of a mother. That's who I was before kids, and it's who I am still today. My children will always come first, but my career will never come last. And maybe one day, I won't have to fight so hard to make time for it.

SURE, I'M A PAINTER

For a long time, my son thought I was a painter. He believed that when I left our house early in the morning to catch the train—something that happened once a week or so—I was headed to a studio where I painted landscapes, quietly selecting a palette of colourful acrylics to bring a canvas to life. I found this delightful, but also confusing, because I am a writer.

"I'm going to work tomorrow," I'd tell the kids. This was a warning because I worked from home most days, but occasionally I'd have to trek into the city or a different suburb to visit a client's office. For a period of time, this was a weekly occurrence. "Going to work" meant that at the end of the day I'd be sitting on a commuter train somewhere in the Greater Toronto Area and would subsequently miss dinner and bedtime.

Even though I usually left my clients' offices by five or so, the long trip home on public transit was incompatible with my kids' early bedtime. Sometimes I stopped and bought tuna poke at Union Station—a less sketchy choice than that sentence implies—treating myself to a meal for the long ride home, my headphones playing a steady stream of music to drown out the loud talkers on the train. Other times, I ate a granola bar scavenged from the bottom of my purse, telling myself I shouldn't spend money on takeout. If the train was quiet, I'd read a book.

Those were exhausting days that included up to four hours on public transit, but they were also the closest thing I got to a vacation from the demands of my everyday life of double shifts between work and parenting. Four hours on public transit wasn't exactly desirable, but it did allow me to zone out or close my eyes while my husband handled dinner and bedtime routines back at home. By the time I'd walk through the door, our kids would be asleep and the dishes would be done. Sometimes this brought on a sense of longing or guilt; other times gratitude and relief. But it was important to me that the kids not be caught off guard by my absence at bedtime, so I'd always let them know when I'd be gone.

"Okay," my son would answer with a smile. "Are you going to do a painting?"

"No," I'd reply, confused. "I'm going to do some writing. I'm going to work."

"Oh, okay." He'd shrug and we'd move on, both a little puzzled. This scenario repeated itself several times before I finally nailed down the source of my son's confusion.

"What do you think Mommy's job is?" I quizzed him.

"I dunno. Writing? And painting."

"Painting? Like art?" I asked.

"Yup," he replied. "Like how you did all the paintings in my room."

Oh, yes—those. The paintings. He wasn't wrong—there were at least six of them in his room—a set of paint-and-sip masterpieces I'd made while drinking wine with friends over the course of several weekends. A local artist had walked us through her process as we happily chugged not-good Chardonnay from a box and painted up a storm.

This is a rite of passage for many moms: you have a drink or two, you make a thing, you go home and show off your work to your family, who then have to pretend your art is good. Sometimes the paintings actually turn out kind of well—probably because of all the help the paid artist offers— while other times your rendering of an oversized bonfire on a beach looks more threatening than relaxing. I am reasonably good at trees and clouds now but cannot paint ocean waves to save my life. It also helps that the artist—always the same one, a whisky-scented, smoky-throated woman of about forty-five who reminds me of Janis Joplin—tells us all we're amazing. She says this convincingly, though it is certainly not true. But this is why we pay her. This, and for the boxed wine.

These events are open to everyone, but each one I've attended has been dominated by women in their thirties and forties, most of whom have children at home. I usually show up with a small group of friends, but by the end of the evening we've morphed into one large social group, wandering around the room, sipping our wine, and complimenting each other's paintings. The mood is decidedly positive; this is a place of encouragement. If you say something negative about your own painting, six women will leap at you with aggressively kind feedback. It's where the mom friends you know and the mom friends you've just met converge for a mash-up of art therapy and happy hour. I love it.

The moment my paint brush touches the canvas, I feel calm and focused. The busyness in my head subsides as I fixate on getting the colours right and the brush strokes just so. I go over every detail, hiding mistakes and adding specks of light. I watch the artist carefully, mimicking the way she drags her brush across the canvas with the perfect balance of deftness and strength. Sometimes I call her over, asking her to demonstrate a certain technique up close. I'm all in and she knows it, and she treats me more warmly than those who pick up their phones as frequently as their brushes. The results of my painting adventures don't always reflect my dedication, but the act itself is the reward.

My son took a liking to these wine-night paintings and insisted on hanging many of them in his room, where they line the walls like a gallery of mediocre, local-restaurant-style art. There's a deep-red cardinal shown in profile, a tent pitched by a lake, a set of footprints on a snowy hillside, a woodsy path between birches at sunset. One shows a tire swing hanging from an oak tree at dusk, a red bike leaning against the trunk. The tree is one of the best I've done, but the rope of the tire swing is too short and would be totally useless in real life. "You're a very good painter, Mama," my son tells me occasionally, admiring my work from his single bed, a dinosaur blanket spread carefully across his lap. I thank him, amused but also pleased that he likes them so much.

My son thinks I'm a painter because that's what he thinks I'm good at. He has never read anything I've written or seen me in a professional situation, but he knows that sometimes I leave the house and come back with art I've created while away. Thus, I'm a painter—and it's true, I guess. Why not? He's identified something about me that isn't entirely wrong. Does it matter if I rarely paint on my own, or it doesn't pay the bills? It isn't how I describe myself—I'm a writer, a wife, a mom, a city person displaced to the suburbs—but I'm also not *not* a painter. My son sees this. He knows me well and sees me in a way that is almost uncomfortably honest.

Growing up, my ambitions were divided between the very corporate (law school, maybe politics) and the somewhat whimsical (writer, artist, baker, bookshop and café owner who sings backup in a band). I dreamed about owning a bed and breakfast, but only so I could decorate the charming rooms, prepare fancy breakfasts, and spend my downtime reading on a shady wraparound porch with a view. I spent little time considering the administration, marketing, and upkeep of such an undertaking—I'd been too busy sourcing vintage quilts and dressers to comple-ment my Farrow & Ball paint scheme.

There is a point in life where passions become hobbies because they just aren't practical. Or maybe I just gave up too soon. Maybe I *should* buy a B&B, I sometimes muse. Maybe that's how I'll retire—making soup in a rural kitchen, pouring coffee and playing host to guests, tending to the garden in the afternoon. My husband, his beard wiry and grey, would mow the lawn, homebrew strong beers in the garage, and tinker around in a woodshed. The kids would visit, eventually bringing their own families to stay, so we'd add a small playhouse in the yard. That wouldn't be a bad way to live out our golden years.

But I'm not an early riser, so we'd only be able to offer guests brunch. And honestly, I'm a good cook, but I'd hate to have to prepare food for strangers on demand. They'd probably be better off with takeout. I do love to garden on cooler days, but often avoid it completely once the temperature rises and my heat rage kicks in. I know I'd grow tired of the responsibility of a large property and would have little patience for loud or demanding guests. The more I think about it, the more I realize how much I'd hate having strangers in my house, even though that is the literal point of owning a bed and breakfast. Also, I would never survive in a rural area. Otherwise though, the plan is solid.

Some dreams aren't meant to be more than just that. But becoming a painter—pouring myself into making art, however unoriginal and mediocre—feels like a wonderfully attainable dream.

I love my life and am happy with the choices I've made, but I also like my children's interpretations of who I am. They see the intimate instead of the polished, the joy instead of the paycheque. They think I'm capable of anything. I hope this is because that's how I look at them, with their happiness at the forefront, their potential constantly shining through. They really could be anything, and maybe so could I.

A set of acrylic paints gathers dust in the corner of my office. Piled beside it are bits of cloth and yarn to make needlepoint floral patterns. A set of watercolours, a sketch book, and unsharpened pencils. Things I've collected because they make me happy. Things I need to use more because it feels good to quiet my brain and make something pretty.

Our kids may not see us the way we see ourselves—or how we think we present ourselves to the world—but they often see us in ways that are meaningful. They see us without the harsh judgment we extend to ourselves and other adults, with the loving eyes of someone who has very little context for comparison. My daughter thinks I'm an excellent baker. Both kids would say I'm a great singer. The truth is that I'm mediocre at both of these things, but I truly enjoy doing them. They see my enjoyment and attach my hobbies to my identity. To the grown-ups in my life, I'm a writer with a background in marketing. To my children, I'm a singing painter who makes exceptional soup and scones. Both of these perceptions are true—I just choose to project one version of myself into the world over any other.

Adult life often forces us to put function before form, and some of our loveliest parts end up on permanent hold or forgotten. Thankfully, our kids see through this and give us permission to be all the things we love, if we can only find the time.

I thought that by being a freelance writer, I'd get to work at something I loved while making money, that I'd basically cheat the system by marrying my creative passion with my need for economic stability. (I confess that my notion of freelance stability was particularly naive.) Of course, I wasn't entirely right—I have to do a ton of corporate projects to stay afloat, many of which I am not passionate about in the least—but I wasn't entirely wrong either. A lot of the work I do provides great creative fulfillment. It's satisfying and I feel spoiled for being paid to do it. I really am doing what I love—just not all the time. And so, there are gaps to fill.

Our go-to paint-and-sip artist ultimately closed her studio and moved four hours away, her own dream crushed by the reality of owning a small business in a tough economy. She had created a beautiful space that made people feel good, but it wasn't enough to stay afloat, so after three years of wine and painting, she left. I wonder what her next move will be: starting again in a new town, chasing another creative goal, or giving in to whatever pays the bills. In my mind's eye, she rebuilds and finds the success she couldn't capture here. I can't imagine her working in an office; she's not meant to sit at a desk. But life is hard on those who follow passion instead of cash. What we think will make us happy doesn't always do so or leave us financially secure.

Bake the scones, sing the songs, make the paintings and hang them proudly. Do all the things that calm the busyness inside your head. Be the version of yourself your children see when you're being happy instead of productive and remember how good it feels when you indulge yourself. Some dreams aren't meant to come to life, but we need to hold on to enough of them to feel alive anyway.

Motherhood is a season that's largely devoted to others, which means carving out time and space to indulge yourself is more important than ever. These are the moments that remind us of who we've always been, long before we were moms; though, ironically, it's often my kids who are there to remind me of this.

WATCH ME HOLD A GRUDGE

To write about the times I've practised forgiveness in my life would be a dramatic missive of wrongs and subsequent recoveries, told entirely from my perspective and thereby completely unfair to every other party involved. I'd include momentary annoyances, like when my sister accidentally destroyed a book she'd borrowed because she decided to read it near water, and weird stuff like when a girl from my elementary school put my pet hamster in her pocket and took it home with her after a play date. (The hamster was eventually returned unscathed by her humiliated father.)

I've been given plenty of grace for my own missteps and failures. None of us is perfect, and we all deserve a little kindness and latitude from time to time. I want to teach this to my children, to help them become the kind of people who hold space instead of grudges.

Forgiveness is good! But I've also come to realize that I'm the kind of mom who never forgets. I say this, and I mean it with my whole heart—if you mess with my children, you are dead to me. (I promise I model empathy and kindness with my outdoor voice.)

There was a stretch of time when my kids seemed particularly busy, and some days I struggled to keep up. My daughter had started junior kindergarten and my son, a rambunctious preschooler, accompanied me to three o'clock pick up every afternoon. On any given day, a dozen or more kids would hang around the schoolyard for an hour or so, scaling the climber or playing games on the field as their guardians looked on. My son spent most of that time running around the playground like a bat out of hell and climbing everything, safety be damned. He was a highly energetic, frighteningly agile child, but like most kids his age, his impulse control skills were "emerging." (Read: he sometimes pushed or hit other kids, despite my constant pleas for him to "use your words" instead.)

As the mother of a hands-on child, I quickly morphed into a broken record. "Our hands are not for hitting!" I'd say as he smacked a kid who took his toy. "Let's give that friend some space," I'd suggest as he enthusiastically got up in another kid's face to tell a story. "I'm so sorry, is he okay?" I'd ask the parent of whichever child my kid had just run into in the park. "Can you say, 'Sorry!' to this friend? They didn't like it when you jumped on them like that." I repeated this to my son, trying to simultaneously instill the importance of consent and owning one's actions while practising the art of apologizing. Some days parenting requires a lot of deep breathing.

Those preschool years were particularly busy, and I had to try my hardest. With two kids only a year and a half apart in age (and one whose natural speed was a hundred kilometres an hour), a husband who worked long hours and had what felt like an equally long commute, and a freelance writing career I worked on at night, I had a lot to manage. We had just moved into our second house, and I'd begun to make friends in the neighbourhood but didn't have a strong social network yet. I spent a lot of time running in circles, and while I was by no means a perfect mother, I was attentive and actively tried to manage my wild child's behaviour. Sometimes I succeeded, other times I failed (usually because I'd dared to pay attention to my other child or attempt conversation with an adult).

One day after school, once the crowds had weeded out somewhat, a group of kids started running in circles around a small, vine-covered pergola standing beside the gym doors. The wooden structure is surrounded by a series of knee-high landscaping stones, and kids tend to use the flat, rocky surface as a racetrack (except when the rocks are inhabited by bees—there are often bees). While most of the children were kindergarten students, there were a few younger siblings in the mix, including my delightfully energetic son. I stood there taking in the sounds of happy shouting and laughter as the kids bounced from stone to stone, circling the pergola. A few parents called out for them to slow down or be careful, but no one made a move to stop their game. My son's face was lit up in excitement when suddenly he sped up and sharply knocked into another small child as he passed with a toddler-size bodycheck, sending him off the rocks and into the grass below. Within seconds, a wail rose from the boy on the ground.

Why did my son do it? I don't know—he wasn't mad or even annoyed, but it definitely wasn't an accident. He was over-excited and, like many three-year-olds, lacked judgment. The boy was upset but physically fine. I immediately removed my son from the game and went to where the boy and his dad were crouched in the grass. "I'm so sorry—" I started, embarrassed.

The dad looked up with an icy expression. "That was vicious," he snapped as his son rose to his feet and ran off, unharmed. "Like, I was watching and that was totally unprovoked."

I paused, taken aback by his anger. "I'm sorry," I started again, now flustered. "He just turned three and we're really working on the hands-off stuff."

The dad crossed his arms and shook his head, unsympathetic. "He shoved him for no reason."

"I know," I agreed. "I just wanted to let him apologize and make sure your son was okay. It looks like he is…"

The dad was unmoved, glaring down at my wide-eyed, twenty-five-pound toddler like he'd just stabbed his son. "Honestly, it was vicious. You've gotta watch him better."

"Oh," I managed quietly as the dad walked away, shaking his head in disgust. I could feel hot tears rising from behind my sunglasses and was immediately furious with myself and everyone around me. Why hadn't I stopped my son before he pushed the boy? Had I not moved fast enough? Should I have even let him run around and get hyped up in the first place? What kind of mother can't stop her child from playing rough all the time? Everything inside me screamed that I had failed, and on top of it all, I felt a sudden hatred for that dad and his total lack of understanding.

It wasn't cool that my son had pushed his child—he and I agreed on that front—but had his own kid never made a poor choice or behaved imperfectly? Had he forgotten that toddlers have minimal impulse-control skills? Had he not seen me there, watching closely and reacting right away? Where did he get off making me feel like a terrible mother when I tried so hard, all the time, every goddamn day?

I am certain the dad at the school park forgot about the incident within days of it happening (or, at least, he never gave any further indication that he thought my toddler was a monster). This makes sense, because it was a two-minute interaction at best. But on my end? Oh, man. He'd kicked me when I was down, and I fucking hated him for it.

I was mad because my son had behaved incorrectly. But I also knew he was a lovable, slightly bananas three-year-old who was still learning boundaries and figuring out how to navigate the world around him. He'd done something bad, but he wasn't inherently bad. The difference is enormous. Children make mistakes; it's how they learn and grow. If they were born with heaps of knowledge, impulse control, and adult reasoning skills, they wouldn't need us parents there to guide them. What we don't need is people shaming us for totally normal childhood behaviour, even when that behaviour needs correcting.

I was mad because I hadn't been distracted, neglectful, or flippant; I was a tired, overextended mom who was doing her damn best. I was teaching kindness and gentle hands, and modelling good behavior, repeatedly explaining why hitting is wrong, involving my toddler in apologies, and poring over resources about how to handle spirited children. I'd spoken with his preschool teachers and a child psychologist to learn new strategies. I'd kept my patience with my son a million times, and yet, after one interaction with this dad, I was done.

"A mom would have understood," I fumed, knowing that wasn't necessarily true. Many dads would have reacted empathetically and plenty of moms would have snapped too. I just hated the father because of how our interaction had made me feel. He didn't care that I'd handled the situation as best I could. He labelled my child, rejected my attempts to reconcile the situation, and walked away before I had the presence of mind to note that my preschooler was not, in fact, vicious, but an amazing yet flawed tiny human—likely not that different from his son.

The mature thing to do might have been to take a deep breath and move on, knowing that one random man's opinion of my family has no bearing on who we actually are. I also could have replied more confidently and said, "Hey, I'm sorry my son pushed you, but he's not vicious. He's young and learning, and I'm doing my best with him."

Instead of doing either of those things, I hid my tears behind my sunglasses, packed up my kids, and sunk into the front seat of my car in total defeat. I called my husband and sobbed. I wiped my mascara-stained cheeks and drove home. Loving your kids is easy, but some days being a mom is hard. That afternoon at the playground, after only a few short words, I was crushed.

In retrospect, I recognize the angry dad at the school was reacting with the same "Hurt my kid, I'll hurt you" instinct I feel deep in my soul. I get it. But here is my confession: it has been several years since this happened, and whenever I see that dad at our kids' school, I may not scowl outwardly, but I sure as hell feel it on the inside. *Fuck that guy*, I think to myself, as if his toddler was the one who shoved mine to the ground. *That judgmental, mom-shaming jerk.*

It's a ridiculous, petty, and totally disproportionate reaction. I've never spoken with him again. I don't know anything about his actual temperament or character. He might be a really nice guy. He may have been having a terrible day himself, or simply been exhausted by his own obligations and stresses. Maybe he was as tired and overextended as me, and he lashed out in a weak moment. I would forgive that in a heartbeat. In fact, I should probably make that assumption and move on. There is zero reason for me to hang on to this grudge, but for whatever reason, I do hold on to it—and as a mom who preaches kindness and empathy, it makes me a total hypocrite.

My children have been on the receiving end of plenty of hits and pushes. Most of the time I'm reasonable in my response, but I've also built a small mental hit list. "I don't like that kid," I've whispered to my husband about a boy who always teased my son. *This kid is sort of an asshole*, I've thought while politely interacting with a tween girl who has repeatedly made fun of my daughter. (Of course she's not actually an asshole, but jeez, leave my kid alone.) I may not have snapped at another parent, but I've judged quietly, made assumptions, and held grudges against parents and children alike. I'm not defending this behaviour and I definitely don't recommend it.

It's impossible not to judge others—as humans, we all do it—but the very least we can do is not judge others out loud. It hurts when someone is mean to your kid, but it's often just as hard to be the parent on the other side of the equation. Very few people celebrate when their child smacks another kid with a toy or pushes someone on the playground. On the contrary, we feel frustration, guilt, and even shame about our abilities as a parent. In my case, I often punish myself more than I'm punished by the parent of whichever child my son has plowed into most recently. If that angry dad hadn't been so critical of me, I would have done it to myself. That's probably why it hurt so much—he was turning the knife I'd already unwittingly placed in my own heart.

I don't want to be that person in someone else's life. No matter how frustrated or judgmental I feel, I make every effort to stop and breathe and not be the jerk who puts someone down in the heat of the moment. I keep negative reactions in my head and out of my mouth. This is such a basic, low-bar goal that I shouldn't even have to put it in writing, but here we are. Empathy can have as large an impact as an insult does, but with a much better long-term result.

I remember how terrible I felt sitting in my car that day, wiping my eyes as my bewildered children looked on from the back seat. I ask myself why I still irrationally dislike that one dad, who is more of a symbol than a real person now, and resolve to use this incident as a reminder that I can be better—I can be better to others than he was to me that day. I can build people up instead of tearing them down. And some days, when I'm graced with the clarity that time and hindsight bring, I remind myself that carrying resentment from a brief interaction that happened years ago makes me the jerk, not him.

Yes, it's probably time to let it go. I promise, I'm trying.

SEND ME INTO THE WOODS ALONE

The joyful chaos of a family home is something I dreamed of, and it remains the place I'm happiest and most at ease. There's nothing better than puttering around my kitchen while the kids make plasticine animals at the table and my husband wanders in and out of the backyard, commenting on the state of the grass. It's always too dry, a little long, a bit patchy here and there; my husband thinks about the yard more in one afternoon than I have in my entire life. In many ways, domesticity is heaven. It's comfort and warmth and habit, a place of acceptance and abiding love. Home is where the heart is, and my family is what fills my heart.

That said, I regularly fantasize about running off into the woods alone.

I don't want to disappear forever—I'm not looking to shave my head, change my name, and charter a sailboat to whisk me away. I just need a break, not from any one person or thing, but from life, along with the demands of motherhood and marriage and being an adult in the world.

Oh, to sit quietly in a place where no one can find me and demand a glass of apple juice. Somewhere I don't have to feign interest in our lawn's hydration levels. Where there are no bills in the mailbox and silence doesn't mean a room in my house is being destroyed by those very children I love so much. A place with no email, no telephone, and no external expectations. Where I exist, but for no one else.

So into the woods I go, deep in the corners of my mind. There, I find a small, charming cabin that is somehow both abandoned and impressively clean, furnished with a comfortable bed and endless shelves of books. There are no spiders. There is a wood-burning fireplace. Magically, there is a coffee maker and my favourite pottery mug. Outside, a thick blanket of trees with wildflowers scattered below. Maybe a lake. There are no clocks. Most importantly, there are no other people.

I read and sleep and soak in the wondrous freedom to do nothing. Sit with my thoughts, or don't think at all. Rest with my back against a tree, drinking in rich solitude unlike anything I've felt in years. Sketching plants and writing poems despite not being particularly skilled at either of those things. Doing them anyway. Watching the sun rise and set against the horizon, nothing else for miles but peaceful, open space. I'd cry at some point, but not out of sadness—just a few elegant, therapeutic tears to signify how good seclusion feels, the kind of gentle tears a young actor cries upon winning an award—heartfelt, touching, but not enough to ruin her makeup.

It doesn't matter what the cabin looks like, and it doesn't matter that it's not real. What matters is the feelings: the freedom and the nothingness. The space and quiet. Gratitude. The blissful absence of decision-making. I crave it, like so many of us do, though its pull ebbs and flows with the stress of my everyday life.

But even my fantasies are rigorous in their demands. For this scenario to truly please me, it needs to be more robust. There must be specific details in place to mollify my anxiety and remove any burden of guilt. My family isn't gone and does not miss me; they're safe and happy, knowing I'll be right back. I've stepped away, but I'll soon walk through our front door again. The freedom isn't in walking away from a life I don't want—I want my life so, so much—it's in pausing it.

My happiness in this fantasy is contingent on the guarantee that I'll wrap my arms around my children again; I'll go back home and feign interest in the grass and wipe the kitchen counters in my usual slow, rhythmic motion. I'll make school lunches and toss another load of towels in the laundry while going over a grocery list in my head. And I'll be content doing these tasks, because they're all a part of a greater picture: a life of chaos and love that wouldn't trade for anything. My family is my bliss.

And yet it's so goddamn normal to need to escape sometimes. We all need a cabin in the woods to head to—both literally and figuratively.

Mothers are flooded with constant needs—from their kids, their partners, their work, the world around them, and, waving meekly in the background, their own basic requirements. Motherhood is a constant juggling act of invisible tasks and emotional labour that knows no bounds. When I walk across a room, I'm asked to stop to get someone a glass of apple juice, even as I'm reading the mail, deciding what to make for dinner, and mentally planning our next dentist visit... Until I step on a Lego and yelp in pain.

When I sit down and look at my phone for a minute while my kids play happily nearby, I feel like a terrible mom. How dare I look at my phone when my beautiful children are right there? (They're always right there.) As Good Moms, we've been trained to feel bad when we're not actively engaging with our kids—but oh, how we're always actively engaged. I engage all the damn time, from the moment my eyes open until the second I collapse into bed at night. I am every tired, busy, loving mom. How could I not crave respite? If I were a machine, I'd break down from the relentless drive of it all. Sometimes I do. And so, when I can, I sit quietly for a moment and dream of the woods.

Sometimes I go there for real. Not exactly as I dream it, of course—I don't have access to a magical secret cabin that's clean, empty, and well-stocked with coffee and books—but I do what I can to create little escapes. Sometimes it's a weekend away with friends; other times it's a conference that is decidedly not a vacation, and yet, because it provides a break from caretaking and family life, it sort of is. I've made room for genuine breaks when I need them, however brief or close to home they may be. This is the product of being the mother of slightly older children, and also of having hit a wall several years ago. My kids need love and care, but it doesn't always have to come from me. They have another parent, other people who love them. I can skip bedtime, sneak off to a coffee shop by myself on a Sunday afternoon, go to a concert, or leave them with a grandparent for the day. I can sleep in on the weekend. I'm not a bad mother if I do things for myself. I've always known this but, for whatever reason, chose to ignore it for too long. I was always there, always on, always mothering—until finally, I allowed myself to step back for a moment. When the world didn't end, I did it again. These days, I feel only moderately guilty about creating this space for myself—and honestly, when it comes to self-care, that's good enough for me. I need to mother myself too.

Escape, then come back. Walk away, but not too far. Love your family hard, but don't forget to make space to love yourself. It took me so long to learn this, but now I'm here to say to you that it's okay. Take an ounce of time for yourself—in fact, take more—and know that everything is going to be just fine when you come back.

ALL TRAGEDY IS YOURS

At the end of a long day, I sink into relaxation on the couch, a warm drink in my hands as I debate between television and silence. My husband sits down beside me and makes the decision for us, turning on the TV almost unconsciously. I didn't need it on, but I don't mind. He flips to the same channel he always ends up on and gives it approximately twenty percent of his attention, as one does when they're tired and aimless. It's just sound, and we sit in quiet companionship until one of us has a thought worth sharing.

The local news station is telling the story of a child who needs a stem cell transplant. She is a little girl—only a toddler really, and somewhat small for her age—with blond hair and round, shiny cheeks. She smiles for the camera but is visibly sick. She probably has tantrums, a special stuffed toy, and a favourite type of yogourt. Her parents appear on the television screen for a few moments, pale and stricken by the gravity of the situation, their hands clasped in their laps as they speak. They are dressed in casual clothes and haven't done themselves up for the camera, their new reality leaving no space for vanity. They've probably aged ten years in a month. Quietly hopeful, the parents are asking the community for help. Everyone is a potential donor, they say, and a cheek swab is all it takes to find out if you're a match.

I turn my head away, refusing to think about the child or the parents. I'm already on the national donor registry and I've never been called. It's been years. The world has never been fair, but some days it seems almost deliberately cruel. These parents should be worrying about potty training and how to get blue marker out of a couch cushion, not finding a stem cell donor for their toddler. Later, during a commercial for a children's hospital, my eyes turn glassy from tears I refuse to allow to fall; upstairs, my children sleep peacefully, their cells healthy and strong. My throat burns in a familiar way as I hit mute in a shameful act of self-preservation.

It's in these moments I realize sadness has a literal weight you can feel throughout your body. It rests on your chest like a brick. Even when the source of grief isn't your own, you might find yourself holding on to it, shifting it between your hands while wondering if there's some way to break it down. If it were yours, you might treat it differently, but this sadness belongs to someone else. You're just borrowing it, uselessly, because it takes nothing away from what those parents feel. It's a pain that feels both meaningful and fruitless all at once.

There was a time when the news didn't make me cry. Back then I was more emotionally detached; I could feel sympathy without being swallowed by someone else's grief. That ended the moment I became a mother. Every tragedy is mine now, and yours too. When one of us hurts, we all hurt.

I feel it when I see a refugee family on the news, living through circumstances I'll never come close to understanding. I cannot fathom the trauma they've been through or the decisions those mothers and fathers and children have been forced to make. I want every family to be able to sit in their pyjamas and watch cartoons together on a Sunday morning or argue about when bedtime is on a school night, not walk through war zones and cross borders on foot in a desperate attempt to find peace and a better life. I want to see their children eat ice cream cones in a park on a sunny day. I want to see their children playing beside my children.

I feel the weight of grief when I pass food or money to a homeless person and feel it again when I walk by someone else on the next street over, offering nothing because my purse is empty. "I'm sorry," I say. "I don't have anything." I mean it, but we both know it's a lie. I have everything, while they sleep on the street.

Motherhood has made me strong, but it's also made me fragile in ways I didn't anticipate. World tragedy feels magnified, from war to natural disasters to climate change. I see the world my children will inherit, and it shakes me to my core. A plane crash over the ocean isn't just sad in a remote way: the immeasurable impact of collective loss hits me viscerally. All those people gone, each with family and friends who loved them. They were someone's parent or child. It's not that I didn't care before, it's just that I can't stop caring now. I can look away or hit mute, but I still feel it all.

I think of that little girl who needs a stem cell transplant as I load the dishwasher the next day, wondering how many people had their cheeks swabbed in an attempt to help. I wonder how her treatment is going and if there will be an update on the news. I wish my phone would ring, telling me I'm a match. It doesn't even need to be her specifically, because she's only one of so many. Any match would do. Still, her face comes back to me as I rinse glasses and plates, knowing how lucky I am to be faced with this boring, domestic task while her parents go through hell. I start making dinner, lost in my thoughts until I'm distracted by a request for chocolate milk. Unlike the girl's parents, I can step away. Yet another example of how life isn't fair.

My daughter comes home from school one day, tossing her backpack onto the ground and asking for a snack. I ask how her day was and she shares a few of the usual recess and gym class anecdotes before pausing, her face solemn. "One of my friends had a hard day," she explains, naming the child. "Her mom has breast cancer. She told us and she was crying because she's scared. She might need an operation and stuff."

The news catches me off guard. I know that mom in the loose yet familiar way you know the other parents at your child's school; we say hello as we pass each other on the blacktop, and my kids often stop to pet her dog. We aren't good friends, but we're friendly, and I like her. I've often wondered how she always looks so calm and put together when I can barely manage to wash my hair. I view mothers like her as somewhat supernatural. And yet: she has cancer. I picture her sharing this information with her two young daughters, which makes me feel genuinely sick for them all. I wonder how she's coping, how her husband is doing, what her prognosis is. I ask my daughter a few gentle questions, trying to toe the line between respecting the mom's privacy and my genuine desire to know if she's okay. She stays on my mind for hours, another heaviness I can't seem to put down, though that's nothing compared to what she's experiencing.

This is the innate emotional burden of motherhood: holding all of the world's tragedies in your hands, whether you want to or not. It's knowing that every child could be your own, every parent could be you. There is a deeper side of empathy I didn't know until I was a parent, and I am filled with it every day.

It's hard. But this empathy is a privilege that brings new depths of joy as well as sadness, and I wouldn't ever deny its importance or wish it away.

Another day, another collapse onto the couch with my husband at my side. The news plays another story about a refugee family who has fled war—but this time, there's a happy ending. The family has settled into a new life in Canada. The father has found work and the mother has been welcomed into the community by neighbours and a group of moms from the local elementary school. They have a modest apartment that is safe and warm, and their children are thriving. Everyone looks healthy and relaxed. The kids are shown laughing and playing, goofing off for the camera the way children do. My heart swells for this family, and I'm overcome with gratitude and relief.

This experience has been repeated in different ways throughout the years. Walking across the parking lot at our local community centre one afternoon, I notice a car painted in rainbow colours. "I beat childhood cancer!" is written across a back window in bright, celebratory paint. Words like *warrior* and *survivor* mark the other windows, along with sunshine, hearts, and rainbows. The car belongs to the parents of a little girl on my daughter's soccer team—a small child who was diagnosed with leukemia as a toddler and has never known anything else. I begin to cry. She's in remission. The years of her life could be counted on one hand and most of them have revolved around blood tests, hospital stays, and chemotherapy. Her parents had been through unimaginable hardship just to keep her alive, and now her family was celebrating because they'd made it out the other side.

It's easier, for some reason, to focus on tragedy, but there are good stories everywhere we look. An older child is adopted after years without a family. A teen comes out to his dad, who supports him and tells him he is loved. A child with neurological differences is welcomed by classmates and told that he belongs. A couple conceives a child after years of infertility, finally able to call themselves Mom and Dad. A new generation fights for justice and social change. I watch it all unfold with optimism, storing up hope and comfort for all the times I'll need to draw from that reserve.

Empathy is complicated, especially when it feels boundless. I've always felt emotions deeply, but now each feeling is intricately connected to motherhood in a way I can't control. It's a heavy load to carry, but it's also invaluable. As much as I feel the weight of this grief and sorrow, I'm also uplifted by collective joy. I hope the feeling can translate into a gentler approach to conflict, a more helpful spirit, and a conscious kindness in the world. All tragedies are ours, but so are all joys—if we let them in. And if we can harness those feelings of grief and love into action and support for others? Magic.

That mom, the one my daughter told me about after school one afternoon? She's doing much better now. It wasn't easy—she demonstrated a strength few of us ever have to muster—but she survived. She appears to be thriving. We still say hello on the blacktop and my kids still stop to pet her dog. From the outside, it looks like her life has gone back to normal, though I'm sure it's anything but. She continues to be more put together than I ever am. When I see her with her children, everything seems right in the world, and, breathing deeply, I let myself believe in the good again.

YOUR PARENTS WERE NEVER OLD

When I was a child, I looked at my parents the same way many other children do, assuming them to be far older and more knowledgeable than they actually were. After all, when you're five or six years old, all adults appear to be old and somewhat worldly (or, at least, more worldly than you, a person who spends much of their day trying not to eat glue in kindergarten). They turn impossibly large numbers on every birthday. They know what time it is, how to drive, where things are, and what the people on the news are talking about, which makes them look infallible, almost omnipotent. Your parents seemed powerful. And absolutely, definitely old.

It didn't occur to me for some time that my parents were actually quite young when I was born. I don't think I fully understood this until I was an adult myself, contrasting their life's timeline with my own and wondering why I didn't see it sooner. My mom was twenty-one when she married my father, who was only twenty-three himself; I was born less than two years later. My sister came along when Mom was twenty-five, and a year and a half later our brother was born. What followed was a series of good times and challenges through which my parents were increasingly misaligned, some bad choices, and, eventually, a great divide that was never reconciled. They separated when I was ten years old, and my mother, then a thirty-three-year-old single parent to three school-aged children, moved us from the suburbs outside Toronto to a small town in Haldimand County, about thirty minutes away.

I was hard on my mother after the divorce, and angry at my father. He moved in with one of his parents who lived three hours away and rarely contacted us in the wake of their split, leaving my mom to deal with the fallout. She commuted to work, leaving early in the morning and getting home just in time for dinner, which was usually a can of cream-based soup poured over chicken or pork and served atop a bed of Minute Rice, which I now think of as the official food of divorce. Our new town was small and felt stuck in a cruel past: both acid-washed jeans and casual racism were accepted as part of the local culture. I was furious that my family was broken and our whole lives had been turned upside down, and that my parents were more human than I'd ever believed them to be. More than anything, I was furious that I couldn't control anything. It was like hurtling down a hill with no brakes—but even worse, because I was sitting in the passenger seat, unable to steer.

I felt abandoned by both of my parents, unwanted and betrayed, and I made sure they knew it. My siblings and I were adjusting to a new school and life as latchkey kids in a rural community and navigating the reconfiguration of our family. We missed our father, but when we saw him, it was tense and emotionally draining, which left us all in sad, volatile states. In time, he rented an apartment a thirty-minute drive away from our new house, but we'd still go weeks or months without seeing him. My mom, desperately needing a break, would beg him to take us for a weekend, usually to no avail. She was hard-working and devoted to us, but not always engaged or present. She also started dating a man I instantly hated and refused to interact with, even when he stayed overnight at our house. And when my father did bring us to his apartment on a Friday night, he'd pick us up around dinnertime and return us to our mother before lunch on Saturday. All three of us would sleep in the living room of his one-bedroom apartment. Instead of bookcases, he had a series of milk crates stacked on the floor next to the drafting table he used for work. A faded maritime flag hung over a window instead of curtains, and the serviette holder on the kitchen table was stuffed with fast-food napkins. We spent most of our time there watching TV. It was probably just as depressing for my dad as it was for us. After a few years, we stopped spending the night, visiting instead for dinner and then leaving shortly after.

I'd love to say that we settled into a better life after a few months or a year, that my mom and dad embraced a fresh start as co-parents and friends, but that never happened. Instead, there were court dates about child support and explosive fights on all sides. Sometimes we saw my dad, sometimes we didn't. We moved again, but for me, our houses never again felt like home. My mother took on all the responsibilities of parenting as we finished elementary school, went through high school, and moved on to university. Now we're all in our thirties and no longer require parenting. And that's that, I guess.

It would be naive to think my childhood experiences didn't affect the choices I've made in relationships and parenting. I obsessed over what went wrong in my parents' marriage and vowed not to let history repeat itself: I'd give myself a better start, make smarter choices, wait until I was at least thirty to settle down. I'd build my own life before letting someone else in and stand tall on my independence.

And then I broke every boundary I set for myself. I fell in love with my husband when I was twenty, got engaged at twenty-four, and married a year later. Still, I told myself we should wait a few years before having kids—two years at least—because I'd be a better mother if I established a career first, paid off my student debt, maybe bought a home. I wanted to be in a position to offer my kids everything they needed, even if I didn't entirely know what that meant. My husband agreed, and then we quickly changed our minds. I was pregnant eight months after our wedding, welcoming our baby home to a one-bedroom apartment on Dupont Street in Toronto, just behind the railroad tracks. My career was an inconsistent patchwork of freelance writing gigs that I cobbled together month after month. I had zero job security and no benefits. And yet everything felt right. I loved my husband, my baby, and my life. I blew off my self-imposed rules because I felt like I was meant to be a mom, no matter how I'd told myself to wait.

In some respects, parenting is a full-blown rebellion. It's judgment transformed into love, worrying all the while that we'll inevitably turn into our parents one day. All the ways I felt frustrated with my own parents growing up are reflected in my mothering. I sit with my children and help with their homework. I make homemade meals and engage with them at the dinner table every night, even when they're tired and grumpy and end up storming off, annoyed with my commitment to this ritual. I read books, sing songs, and bake muffins with them. I connect with their teachers, get to know their friends, and acknowledge their feelings. I discipline calmly and firmly (or try to—my husband may disagree, having heard me at both my best and my worst).

I've built loving family traditions, made space for one-on-one time with each of my children, and make myself available whenever they need me. My approach to parenting is more attachment than free range, though I try to strike a healthy balance. I apologize when I've been short-tempered or distracted. I show emotion freely and let them know that it's okay to be sad or frustrated. I'm always, always there for them. My husband is there with me, and when I'm working or go out of town, he slides easily into parenting on his own until I'm back. Our kids never come home to an empty house.

But then, the flipside: I worry my kids don't have the independence or street smarts I had at their ages, that their lives have been too easy and adult-directed. A latchkey kid takes on a lot of responsibility at a young age, but they learn from that. They build confidence and develop advanced decision-making skills. A latchkey kid can walk the neigh-bourhood alone, buy things at a store without an adult, use the stove, and make decisions about whether or not to answer the door when a stranger knocks. They advocate for themselves and are more self-guided. They're tough.

When I was eight or nine years old, we lived a block away from the dance studio where I took ballet, tap, and jazz with a glamorous blond woman named Cheryle and her daughter, who was sixteen and seemed endlessly cool to me. I loved dance. The thing was, my lessons started at four and my parents didn't get home until after five. So I walked to the studio by myself once a week while my younger siblings stayed with a babysitter. All of the other kids arrived with parents in tow—bouncily permed moms helping their daughters in and out of their leotards and tights—and most of the parents stayed to watch. Not me: I rolled in by myself, danced, and then walked out the door on my own, sometimes stopping at the convenience store to buy penny candy for the three-minute walk back to my house. I don't remember any of the parents asking where my mom and dad were, but they must have wondered. Or maybe not. It was the early nineties, after all, when we all rode bikes around the neighbourhood until the street lights came on. The other parents may have been more jealous than concerned. I'll never know.

By the time I was eleven—my parents then living sepa-rate lives—I had taken public transit alone, dealt with re-pairmen while my mother was at work, and taken a cab to my family doctor's office while home sick from school with strep throat. I was used to filling out school forms for myself and my siblings, and sometimes took my mother's credit card to the store to pick up groceries. I cooked (but didn't clean, my mother would point out). I'd learned to reset a blown fuse in the basement and taken my younger brother to the emergency room after he hit his head while

I was in charge (I asked an older neighbour to drive us to the hospital). Whatever adult stuff needed doing I did, because I was the adult. And I didn't hate it! I liked being an independent kid with a house key and hours upon hours of unmonitored time. I didn't know anything different, and at the end of the day, I didn't feel neglected. I knew I was loved—I also just had more freedom and responsibility than most of my peers.

How will my kids learn these skills if I'm always there? They're incredibly smart, but they've never even had a paper route. They've never been to the park alone. I don't want the needle to swing all the way to the other side of the dial.

These days, when my kids ask me to do something for them, however large or small the task may be, I often make a split-second decision between "They should do that themselves" and "Just let them be kids." It's a never-ending internal debate. I wonder what qualifies as normal parenting, and what is overparenting? What counts as advocating for them and what is bulldozing obstacles they could have faced and learned from? I sometimes question if I talk to their teachers too much, because I have no real sense of how parents and teachers should interact. When I give them more freedom, it always feels like neglect, until I see them thriving; then my mindset adjusts. When I make them a snack when they ask me to, knowing full well they could easily make it themselves, I wonder if I'm nurturing them or hindering their independence. I rarely feel confident in my decisions, forever viewing myself as both too doting and not doting enough. Yet somehow I know I'm a good mom. I'd be easier on myself if I wasn't, I reason.

What's made this easier is time and instinct—mostly on my kids' part. They push for more freedom and like to show me how capable they are. As this happens, I'm forced to follow their lead in order to not hold them back. They're growing and I'm learning along with them. They may not be booking their own dental surgeries like I was, but they also don't need me to hold their hands through every little task. They can be nurtured and still become independent. I can do things for them because it's kind and loving and know it won't lead to them becoming thirty-year-olds who can't fill out paperwork or make themselves a sandwich. Life doesn't need to be hard to make you strong.

Perspective is a hell of a thing, and I realize now that my parents were never as infallible as I originally saw them. They were young and flawed and doing the best with the tools they had. I know more about their own upbringings now, as well as their personal strengths and weaknesses, and understand how they must have clashed in times of stress. I see the pressure and worries that must have clouded them, and how hard they tried—and I remember there were good times too. There is so much context and nuance that children can't understand.

I am far from perfect as a wife and mother, and I'm sure my own children will look back on my parenting and have plenty to critique. Their feelings will be just as valid as my own.

I also know that everything I felt and experienced could be processed completely differently by someone else. The overwhelming waves of anger and pain I was drowning in during the hardest years might have been ridden out easily by someone else. Another child may not have shared the sense of obligation or responsibility that I felt. Not every latchkey kid becomes a second parent in their household. My response wasn't a choice, because it was the only thing I knew how to do. I no longer knew how to be a kid, but I wasn't truly an adult, so I hovered between both worlds.

In every way this was hard; it was also an education. Being thrust into adulthood at such a young age is what shaped my independence and made me who I am. I wouldn't recommend it necessarily, but I don't look back with regret because I'm happy with who I am today. I hope my parents, both thriving in their own ways now, can say the same thing.

The sooner we realize our parents are human, the sooner we can look past their failings and be grateful for what they got right. I don't parent the same way my mother did. Her best and mine are not the same thing, but we are both good moms. I've intentionally oversimplified and skipped over a lot here, but I'll end on a silver lining: With age comes perspective, and along with that, understanding and the ability to forgive. If ever I should need it, I hope my kids will grant me the same.

I DON'T ALWAYS WANT TO SLEEP
THROUGH THE NIGHT

My daughter cries out for me in the middle of the night, her groggy voice cutting through the silence of the dark house. I roll over in bed, my eyes still closed, pausing before leaving the warmth of the covers. It's somewhere between two and four in the morning, that tomblike period of time that falls after midnight but before any specks of light begin to brighten the world behind the curtains. It's quiet, aside from the rhythmic breathing of my husband next to me, so I lie still in the darkness, waiting and listening. I'm still half-asleep and wonder if the sound I heard was part of a dream.

"Mama?" she calls again. So I get up and walk down the hall to her room.

"I had a nightmare about ants," she tells me as I sit on the edge of her bed. This is a very specific fear that often works its way into my daughter's dreams in place of monsters and other usual childhood concerns. "I dreamed there were ants in my room and on my blanket," she continues, a shudder visibly running down her spine. "I want to sleep in your room."

I nod and murmur in sleepy agreement, grabbing her pillow as I stand up. She clutches her worn stuffed lamb and follows me down the hall, our bare feet padding along the wood floors.

My daughter is not a baby anymore, or even a toddler—she is a smart, capable, independent nine-year-old who runs around the neighbourhood unsupervised, aces every math test, and uses the stove with little help. She often reads for hours after I've tucked her in and then turns out her own light, essentially putting herself to sleep. She doesn't need me to rock her to sleep or take her to the washroom in the middle of the night. She brushes her own teeth. Now entering her tween years, she enjoys the privacy of her messy pink bedroom and prefers to sleep in her own bed. This is a rare event.

Crawling back under the covers, I am well aware that I'm about to sleep on a sliver of mattress while my daughter stretches out beside me, her pale limbs splayed about like tree branches. All of the blankets will likely be stolen from me before dawn. I will be tired and achy in the morning, but feeling her curl up on the edge of my pillow, already snoring lightly, I don't dare suggest she go back to her own room. These nights are few and far between now, and each time could be the last.

Every time I have this thought, my throat catches and my heart aches. If I let myself think about it for too long, the ache will turn into hot, ugly tears. I cannot imagine a world where my babies don't crawl into bed with me after a nightmare. And yet here we are, them still so young but suddenly so brave and fiercely independent, and me still their mother, forever wanting to scare away ants and monsters and make everything okay. "I'm here for you!" I want to shout, but they're hardly ever afraid. Nothing prepares you for a time when, after years of desperately yearning for uninterrupted sleep, you'd give anything to have little feet poking you in the ribs all night.

Motherhood is littered with final acts that sneak up on you: the last time your child crawls into your bed in the night, the last time you hold them in your arms while walking down the stairs, the last time you sing them to sleep. The final act of washing their hair in the bath, buttoning up a shirt, or tucking them into bed at night. Carefully applying sunscreen to their baby-soft arms or gently towelling them off after a swim. Turning off the light. You do these things from the day your child is born and for years thereafter, then notice that you're asked to do them less and less, until you finally accept that your children don't need you to do them anymore. They are a thing you used to do, a remnant of the past. Your loving arms will always be there to wrap around your children, but you'll no longer pick them up and walk around with them casually perched on your hip or carry them delicately from the car to their beds as they sleep. Is there anything more heartbreaking than this? As my children grow, I become proud and devastated in equal measure.

I haven't rocked either of my children to sleep in my arms for years now. I don't even buckle their seat belts in the car; instead, I chirp, "Seat belts?" and await an exasperated confirmation that they've buckled in. I spent years encouragingly (and irritatedly) telling my kids they were capable of getting themselves a bowl of cereal or a glass of water, and now they do it. How is this possible? Why didn't I recognize that these final moments were happening until they had passed?

For so many years, the daily grind of motherhood was made up of simple tasks designed to keep my children safe and well. I'd lift them from their beds in the morning and place them there again at night, a million acts of love and service sandwiched in between. I'd offer food because they needed nourishment, and I'd wash them so they'd be clean. Now they make their own sandwiches and shower while I sit nearby, listening to them babble some school-age narrative at me while I wait with a towel. One day soon, I imagine the towel will hang from a hook on the washroom door and I won't be there at all.

I miss some of the gone things. In a way, I miss all of the gone things. I don't want to go back to never sleeping and constantly wiping butts, but I feel the acute loss of the early years, particularly as time marches on and my rose-coloured glasses grow even rosier. I miss the days when motherhood felt like a cocoon that my children and I lived in together, safe and warm and always within each other's reach. I may cherish my new-found mom-of-big-kids freedom, but I miss the constant call to provision. Not just the sense of nurturing and connection it created, or the satisfaction of meeting their needs, but the (often false) sense of control over their well-being. The knowledge that they had what they needed because, largely, I could provide it to them. The world couldn't hurt them because I was there, wrapped around their days like a cloud of maternal strength and love. It felt like it would be that way forever—and then it wasn't.

I see new moms and I want to warn them. Do you know that one day you won't even need that giant diaper bag? You'll just get up and go. Your baby will hop on a bike and disappear around the corner without even looking back. They will have a social life and secrets and conversations you aren't privy to. They won't need a car seat. They will have very strong opinions that don't always match your own. They'll have their own email address!

Mercifully, human growth isn't always linear. It shoots forward and then dips back again, circling around when it's gone too far too fast. My children weigh themselves constantly because they realize that a higher number is an indication of growth. They have no sense of the value society places on different body types or how their own shapes fit into this complicated map. But they did know that when they hit forty pounds, they'd be able to ride in a booster seat instead of a baby seat, and when they reached this milestone they celebrated triumphantly, even though they each hit that weight at a much older age than most of their peers. Their next goal was fifty pounds—just because. They often stand back-to-back, their skinny arms and legs stretched out as long as they can manage, asking if they look taller. Am I bigger? Have I grown?

Always, the answer is yes. You've always grown.

When she is tired or overwhelmed, my daughter tells me that she wants to be a baby again, or maybe a four-year-old. Four-year-olds have fewer problems, she assures me, and lower expectations from society. Tween life is hard. I rock her in my arms and kiss her on the nose, promising that everything will be okay. No matter how old she gets, she'll always be my tiny baby. "And you'll always be my mommy," she replies, comforted. Don't grow out of this, I silently beg her. Please feel this way about me forever, because I will always feel this way about you.

To mother is to be in a constant state of mourning as well as joy. You give all of yourself, all the time, with the goal of watching your child step away into their own life. How far will your heart stretch, you wonder, knowing it will extend to wherever they are.

"Mama," my son often tells me, "I need snuggles." He curls into my lap, his long legs dangling off to the side as he rests his head against my chest.

"Will you always need mama snuggles?" I ask, sounding more and more like the creepily enmeshed mother from that popular children's story—you know the one.

"Yes, even when I'm a grown-up!" my son replies in earnest, having read the book. He doesn't know that he won't want to be held like a baby when he's thirty, but I let us both pretend.

One day his spouse will love me, I know.

Transitions are hard for children, but they also bring heartache to parents. I love my big kids, but I miss the moments I took for granted or wished forward in time. I'd trade the sleep I'm getting now for one more day of being nap-trapped by a fussy baby. I long to hear my daughter's toddler voice mispronounce new words or tell me she "can't know" things. I don't remember the last time she said that.

But every now and then, something I've accepted as lost forever will slip back to me for a moment, and I'll clutch it with all of my might, wanting to remember the feeling forever. It's always a gift. A scary dream about ants gives me one more night with a baby in my bed. I don't know how much longer she'll ask for it, but when she does, I'll be there.

BABIES ARE GOING TO SMASH THE PATRIARCHY

I've decided the helplessness of youth is a myth. How could it not be? Just look at children—their energy, their unbridled emotion, the optimism of minds that haven't had time or reason to grow jaded. Despite the tantrums and need for daily naps, there is nothing helpless or insignificant about children. They are small, but they've got power. Kids have years ahead of them filled with boundless potential; they're not clay to be moulded, but rivers that will run wild and free. Their lives won't be easy, but what they do might be incredible. I look at my kids and, while there are so many reasons to feel trepidation, again and again I choose hope. I have to—otherwise, what have I done? What selfishness led me to bring new life into this messed-up world? I don't just want better for them, I need better for them. I can't bear to imagine the alternative.

I'm well aware of the divide between the future I want to believe in and the future that's likely to arrive. I'm imaginative but not naive. Some days I feel a deep sadness about the world my children have been born into, where despite decades of talk about "doing better," there is still poverty and war and piles of single-use plastics in every goddamn household. World leaders aren't leading. There are children in cages while billionaires visit the moon. It takes riots to garner a small fraction of the justice that's deserved for the people we continually fail. I lie awake at night thinking about all of the bad things out there and feel like my best efforts to stop them aren't even a blip on the global radar. We move a step or two forward, then trip and fall back, then repeat.

I'm grateful for my country when I compare it to others, but not when I test it against my own ethics. The cracks in our brilliant facade are too deep to ignore. There is more talk than action, heaps of praise for ideas rather than tangible results. There's a gulf between the society I want and believe in, and the one I see around me each day. I vote in every single election and the people I vote for have never won.

And then I remind myself that as deeply and genuinely as I care, I'm complicit. That my privilege has allowed me to be blind to countless wrongs, to ignore serious issues and injustices simply because I've never come face to face with them myself and I hadn't bothered to look. I know now that the harms I've experienced and been enraged by are just the tip of the iceberg. Misogyny, but as a white woman. Sexism, but as a cis woman. Economic hardship, but as someone the banks are still willing to offer a mortgage to. I see myself represented in entertainment and media. I had easy access to education. I've never lacked food or shelter. Almost every layer of my identity has made my life easier.

Unconsciously, I've participated in systems of oppression my entire life. I've benefited from my skin colour and the inherent biases of others. I've done this without a second thought, until recent years—which isn't to say I'm not still an active participant, but I'm now trying to participate to a lesser extent. There's a huge difference between equality and equity, and for years I fought for one without thinking much about the other. My feminism hasn't been as intersectional as it should have been. It still isn't, though I'm really trying.

I think I'm a good person. I know my heart is kind. But that doesn't mean I haven't screwed up over and over again. This reflection is uncomfortable to acknowledge and even harder to think about in detail, and it should be. You don't learn anything in a comfortable place. We should all get a little more uncomfortable.

The world I'm raising my children in is a bubble. I haven't done this on purpose, but it's the truth. They have privilege because of where they were born and who their parents are—a white, middle-class married couple with a nice house, two incomes, and one killer benefits plan. Their lives are easier for all that. Hardship isn't distributed evenly. It's arbitrary as hell.

It took a long time for my own bubble to pop, but my children will know more than I did at their age. I will teach them, and they will teach me, and we'll all keep learning together. And hopefully they'll do more; their generation will be better than mine and the ones before. I already see this happening across the world—young environmental activists, teens fighting for stronger gun laws, kids who care more about human rights than many adults. I'm in awe of their words and their values and what they fight for. Parents are taught to fear the teenage years, but when you look at what teens are capable of, there is so much opportunity. Kids are leading the way.

Sometimes this feels like a lot of pressure to put on still-developing people. There are days I think I'd be better off raising my children on a deserted island. I want to hide them from the storm. I think a lot of parents feel this way. How dare we force them to inherit this mess? We've failed so miserably, all of us, for not giving our kids something better. All of this devotion to mothering and keeping them safe, just to send them out into a global dumpster fire. How could we have let so many things go wrong?

But at the same time, I see light ahead. I look at people younger and stronger and often wiser than me doing great things, and I am filled with optimism. I see them reimagining our relationship to the environment, coming together to stand up against harmful policies in their schools and communities, demonstrating acceptance, and advocating for human rights. I believe in them. They are angry, but they are innovative. They are invested in more than themselves. The kids are alright. Babies will grow into leaders and nurturers and people of action. They will throw statues into the sea and create a new world that is kinder and more inclusive. They will lead with love and empathy, and their voices will become the standard, not the dissent.

I want so badly for all of this to be true, not just for my children, but for everyone's.

I want future generations to do better than I have, and I believe they will. But we can't place the burden entirely on them. No matter how bright and capable young people seem, it's still up to us to fight until we are too old and tired to do it anymore. This is still our cross to bear. But, children, I believe in you. Babies are going to smash the patriarchy. I can feel it.

The future won't be simple, and it certainly won't be easy, but I'm already watching our kids with respect and awe. I hope they resist capitalism, erase borders, and strive for both equity and equality. That they find ways to protect our planet, the one we've abused for so long that it feels normal to watch it fall apart. I hope our babies grow up to break glass ceilings and dismantle hateful systems. And before all that, I hope they still get to be children—to play and learn and grow. And that all children get to be children—not just lucky ones like mine.

In a world that often feels cold and wrong, it is because children exist that I remain filled with hope.

PLEASE DON'T GROW UP
TO BE ASSHOLES

My dear babies:

You are my life's greatest joy, and I love you more than you'll ever know. I think you are truly good people—the best people!—and have no doubt that you'll transition into adulthood with the same kindness, curiosity, and compassion you have now.

My dreams for you are simple: to be happy, to live a life that's warm, secure, and fulfilling, with plenty of love. You'll have your own goals, and I'll support them. I can't tell you how to live or who to be, but as your mother, I have just one request: please, don't grow up to be assholes.

Be nice to friends and strangers alike. Value your friendships, love your family, and put goodness out into the world. Give back to your community, learn from your mistakes, and continue to learn and grow. Read books, appreciate art, and listen to music. Take time to notice the beauty all around you. Keep a sense of humour, but not at the expense of others.

If you see an injured animal on the side of the road, call the nearest wildlife centre and get it the help it needs. Snuggle with puppies and kittens whenever you're given the opportunity. Hold a baby goat as often as possible. Or at least once in your life. Learn to identify birds or at least appreciate how spectacular they are. Seriously, you should feel excited when you see a kestrel or a goldfinch. (But it's okay to shun seagulls. We all know they're the rats of the sky.)

Show compassion to those less fortunate than you. Be an ally and advocate instead of a roadblock. Recognize your privilege and stand up to injustice when you see it. You are going to see it everywhere, and if you don't, you need to look more closely.

If you end up with wealth, share it. Be generous to charities and give awesome presents. Write heartfelt cards to the people you care about, and don't take anyone for granted. Be selfless more than you're selfish, but don't put yourself last. Chase your dreams, but don't crush anyone else's dreams along the way. Lend a helping hand whenever you can and give compliments freely. Punch up, not down.

When you find love, cherish it, and know that you deserve to be treated well. Your father is my best friend, my biggest supporter, and a genuinely good person who makes really cute babies. He isn't perfect, but he's never mean. Also, he always stops at Starbucks when I want a coffee (so, all of the time). That's romance.

Spend time with your grandparents, even when you're busy, because, my God, you're going to miss them one day. Remember other people's birthdays. Know your values and stick with them no matter what. Be open to other perspectives and new information, but never stray from your ethics and who you are. Lead with love.

Don't put other people down to feel better about yourself. Don't be boastful or measure your success by the size of your house, the car you drive, or your bank account. Wealth doesn't equal worth, and it doesn't make someone interesting. I am mentally running through a short list of billionaires right now and, honestly, I wouldn't want to hang out with any of them.

Get an education, but don't assume you're smarter than someone because you have more formal learning experience than they do. This goes both ways—the person who was denied an education could be brilliant, and that guy with three degrees may be an idiot. I know *so many* of those guys, and so will you. Intelligence comes in many forms, and so does its opposite.

Don't be rude to transit workers, servers at restaurants, or retail employees. They work just as hard as someone at a desk for less money, and they don't deserve anyone's condescension or scorn.

Don't judge others on their gender, sexuality, race, religion, economic position, or body type. Don't be that guy who parks in two spaces at the grocery store. No one's car is that special. We all hate that guy.

Don't be the person who plays devil's advocate at every chance. There's a difference between seeing multiple perspectives and intentionally being a jerk. People avoid that person at parties, and for good reason. Parties are supposed to be fun! On that note, always offer to help clean up after a party. They're a lot of work to put on, and even when help is declined, the gesture is appreciated.

Don't think you can trash a hotel room because you've paid for it or leave your dirty tray on the table in a cafeteria after having a meal. Take care of your own damn garbage. The world is not your trash can.

Treat others with respect until they give you a reason not to. Don't be the guy who swears loudly in public or has conversations on speakerphone. Swear words don't belong everywhere, and the only place for speakerphone is in your own house. I hope to God this isn't still a thing people need to learn by the time you're grown up. Don't mock people, especially when you don't know their story. Fight with facts, not petty insults. If you see someone who needs your seat on the subway or in a waiting room, give it to them.

Don't ignore people who are experiencing homelessness or make assumptions about how they got there. You don't know their story and they don't owe it to you. Offer them change or another act of kindness, but never, ever look down on them.

Don't hunt for sport. It's just senselessly murdering a creature that doesn't have access to defence weapons, and it's not cool. Your life won't be made better by shooting a rhino. You're better off punching a billionaire.

Don't hold a grudge or carry hate in your heart, because it will hurt you more than it hurts anyone you're mad at. Your genetic makeup is going to make this particularly challenging, and I'm sorry about that.

Take the high road. You'll never regret it.

Smile at strangers on the street, and always say please and thank you.

Choose a job you think you'll love, and don't be afraid to change course if it doesn't turn out the way you'd hoped. You don't need to be miserable because you feel obligated to stick with a specific career or version of yourself. You will have thousands of opportunities, even if they do feel limited at first.

If you take nude photos, wait until you're older than eighteen and don't show your face. Or fine, show your face if you must, but make sure you're happy with the pictures because these things always get out eventually. The Internet is forever.

Spend time in nature. It's good for you.

Please learn how to cook, clean, and pay your own bills. I'm here to teach you these things, but you need to be willing to learn how to do them. If you eventually hire someone else to do any of these jobs, treat them kindly and tip them well.

Be gentle on your parents. We love you and we did our best.

What this all boils down to is please, please, don't grow up to be assholes. I truly believe that you will always be incredible people, but it's my job to keep you on the straight and narrow. I'll do everything I can to be a good role model and help you become the best people you can be. But if I fail—and I'll probably fail a lot—please look to this list as a guide.

Oh, and remember that I love you. So, so much, forever.

xo Mama

ACKNOWLEDGEMENTS

Thank you to all of the writers and editors who have given me encouragement and opportunities over the years: Lynda Simmons, Shannon Lee Simmons, Julie Cole, Louise Gleeson, Kim Shiffman, Ariel Brewster, Heather Dixon, Jennifer Millard, Katie Bridges, Natalie Milne, Katie Dupuis, Gina Makkar, Sandra E. Martin, and Ann Douglas. Thank you to Ken Murray and Alexandra Shimo for their guidance. Thank you to the teams at *Today's Parent*, *SavvyMom*, *Broadview Magazine*, *Romper*, *Scary Mommy*, *ParentsCanada*, *Reader's Digest*, *MoneySense*, and every other publication that believed in me, hired me, and paid me on time.

There are many other incredible people in the media and writing communities who I forced my friendship on through social media and in real life. Thank you for letting me into your world and giving me advice along the way.

Thank you to my people: my long-time friends, my mom friends, work friends, the court moms, my writer friends, and all the other weird and wonderful individuals in my life. I can't name everyone without this turning into an awkward parody of a high school yearbook, but you know who you are and I love you.

Thank you to everyone who read my work early on and the people reading it now. Thank you to anyone who ever joined a book club, wrote something from the heart, emailed something kind to a writer, or left a positive comment online. Thank you to all the librarians and independent bookshop owners out there, and all of the incredible authors who have inspired me throughout my life.

This book would not exist if Leigh Nash hadn't believed in me and given me an incredible opportunity. Leigh, you're so good at your job, it's almost unfair to other publishers.

Thank you for helping me make something I'm proud of. I am forever grateful for your dedication and skilled guidance.

Andrew Faulkner is a brilliant editor but also a kind and patient friend, and I could not have made this book without him. Andrew, I'm so glad our paths continue to cross in unexpected and wonderful ways.

Thank you to my partners in crime since childhood, Shauna and Craig. You are my best friends and I love you both very much. Thank you to Auntie Donna, cousin Wendy, and the rest of my family on all sides. Thanks to my dad. Thank you to my wonderful in-laws. Thank you to Uncle Don for encouraging me to make writing my career when I wasn't sure it was possible.

I am filled with gratitude to have had so many years of love and encouragement from my grandparents, Don and Mimi Gillies, as well as great-aunts Anne Johnston and Mary Haylock.

Thank you to my mom for her unwavering support, words of motivation, and generosity. I love you and I could not have written this book without your help. Also, please stop asking me if the book is done. It's done now.

Thank you to Adam for your love, support, humour, and patience. I will never not appreciate it when you get me a coffee. I love you and like you a lot. I don't know what possessed us to get married so young but I'm glad we did.

And finally, thank you to my babies, O and H. You are the loves of my life and the inspiration behind so much of what I do. Thank you for laughing when I told you the title of my book and always being in on the joke. Being your mom is the best thing that's ever happened to me.

INVISIBLE PUBLISHING produces fine Canadian literature for those who enjoy such things. As an independent, not-for-profit publisher, our work includes building communities that sustain and encourage engaging, literary, and current writing.

Invisible Publishing has been in operation for over a decade. We released our first fiction titles in the spring of 2007, and our catalogue has come to include works of graphic fiction and nonfiction, pop culture biographies, experimental poetry, and prose.

We are committed to publishing diverse voices and experiences. In acknowledging historical and systemic barriers, and the limits of our existing catalogue, we strongly encourage writers from LGBTQ2SIA+ communities, Indigenous writers, and writers of colour to submit their work.

Invisible Publishing is also home to the Bibliophonic series of music books and the Throwback series of CanLit reissues.

If you'd like to know more, please get in touch: info@invisiblepublishing.com